*Telepathy and
Clairvoyance*

Telepathy and Clairvoyance

Views of some little investigated capabilities of Man

By

W.H.C. TENHAEFF

*Professor at the State University
of Utrecht, The Netherlands,
and Director of the
Parapsychological Institute*

With a Foreword by

Berthold Eric Schwarz, M.D.

*Fellow of the American
Psychiatric Association*

CHARLES C THOMAS · PUBLISHER
Springfield · Illinois · U.S.A.

Published and Distributed Throughout the World by
CHARLES C THOMAS · PUBLISHER
BANNERSTONE HOUSE
301-327 East Lawrence Avenue, Springfield, Illinois, U.S.A.

This Book is a translation
of the original Dutch edition,
Telepathie & Helderziendheid,
published in 1965 by
W. de Haan, N.V., Zeist.

With THOMAS BOOKS *careful attention is given to all details of
manufacturing and design. It is the Publisher's desire to present books
that are satisfactory as to their physical qualities and artistic possibilities
and appropriate for their particular use.* THOMAS BOOKS *will be true
to those laws of quality that assure a good name and good will.*

Printed in the United States of America
H-2

FOREWORD

TELEPATHY AND CLAIRVOYANCE is not Professor Tenhaeff's major work, nor was it intended to be. "The little book," as he modestly terms it, "is only an introduction, to help educated readers and, perhaps, also those less fortunately well-rounded, to understand the nature of certain experiences which may have frightened them. Although such things are not easily tested, nor readily grasped, they are none the less real."

Professor Tenhaeff considers paranormal phenomena—extrasensory perception, including telepathy, clairvoyance, precognition, etc., etc. —to be extensions of normal human abilities. He holds the opinion that everyone possesses paragnostic capabilities but these capabilities do not reveal themselves in all persons in equal degree. There are gradual differences between men. Many say that they have had no paragnostic experiences, but there are also many people who have had from time to time spontaneous telepathic or other paragnostic experiences. Then there is a third category of people who have these experiences regularly; we call them paragnosts and we have not only to study their phenomena but also the structure of their personality. He does not claim that a person can develop them, nor does he pretend to have a method for developing latent abilities.

Even so, knowledge of the nature of paranormal phenomena may do much to help an individual widen his sphere of awareness, and undo the emotional distortions which are not infrequently brought on by misunderstanding or misapprehension. There are, unfortunately, quite a few people who—on the threshold of becoming more aware of themselves and of others in their environment—become afraid and upset instead, because they do not realize the meaning and healthy potentialities of their latent capabilities.

The significance of Professor Tenhaeff's contribution to parapsychology is that he has devoted more than forty-three years to the documentation of paranormal ability in terms of its usefulness to society and to the individuals so endowed. He has delved deeply into the emotional dynamics of psychic experiences. The renowned Gerard Croiset is only one among scores of sensitives to whom Professor Tenhaeff has applied his meticulous investigative procedures, based upon a scholarly background of unequalled breadth and solidity.

This background was not easily acquired. Willem Tenhaeff, who had already expressed an interest in psychical research at the age of 18, was not to matriculate as an undergraduate at the University of Utrecht until the age of 30 (1924)—and then contrary to the expressed wishes of his parents. Nine years later he published his doctoral dissertation and was appointed a free-lance lecturer at the University. This position carried no salary. In the years before the second world war, Dr. Tenhaeff traveled widely, lecturing in numerous other countries in Europe, but his primary activity—as it remains today—was the exploration in depth of the personality structures of persons endowed with psychic—paranormal—abilities. It should be stressed that his research was not confined to the individuals themselves, but led also to investigation of their families, friends, and acquaintances. The results of these qualitative and psychodynamically oriented studies have been published in ten books, of which this is the first to appear in English, and in the Dutch *Journal of Parapsychology* (*Tijdschrift voor Parapsychologie*), of which he was a co-founder in 1928.

The Germans invaded the Netherlands in 1940. Two years later, Dr. Tenhaeff was dismissed from his post at the University and had to flee to escape arrest. He remained in hiding during the balance of the war and passed the time by writing his *Inleiding—Introduction to Parapsychology*. Shortly after resuming his lectures at the University of Utrecht in 1945, he made the acquaintance of a then unknown ex-grocer named Gerard Croiset and began the research which has led to world fame for this individual's talent for locating missing persons. Professor Tenhaeff's studies of Croiset spectacularly demonstrate what wondrous things a human being is capable of.

It was not until 1951, at the age of 57, that Dr. Tenhaeff was officially appointed a teacher on the University payroll. For the first time anywhere in the world, parapsychology had achieved recognition as an accredited subject. Two years later, in 1953, the Netherlands Ministry of Education at the Hague honored Dr. Tenhaeff by creating a professorship in the world's first Chair of Parapsychology and appointing him Director of the Parapsychological Institute of the State University of Utrecht. At last, after thirty-nine years of scholarship, research, sacrifice and courage, lecturing on parapsychology to undergraduates as well as graduate students in medicine and psychology, Dr. Tenhaeff became the Professor of the young science, which, although he would be quick to disclaim it, is so patently his offspring. The Professor, as we shall frequently have occasion to notice in his text, is almost excessively fond of dwelling on the contributions of the "pioneers," some of whom date from the eighteenth century. But it is Prof. Dr. W. H. C. Tenhaeff who, first and foremost, has seen and established the relationships which make of parapsychology an organized field of study not limited to highly stereotyped statistical analyses, but rich in practical applications to everyday situations and in even more significant implications for the future orientation of ideas and the welfare of mankind.

Among the many persons whose assistance has been solicited and freely given for this work, it is my honor to mention first the translator, Cora Matteson-Lauta van Aysma, a lady endowed with quite extraordinary energy and capabilities, who journeyed to Utrecht to undertake this challenging assignment under the personal tutelage of Professor Tenhaeff; her husband Archibald C. Matteson, whose mastery of English prose and editing brought grace and clarity to the manuscript; the late Henry P. Balivet, who brought us together; Adeck and Mieke Land, without whose hospitality in Driebergen the translation could never have been achieved; Gerard Croiset; Jack Harrison Pollack, who most graciously permits us to benefit from his detailed research into the Professor's background, as set forth in his excellent "Croiset the Clairvoyant"; the staff of The Parapsychology Foundation and the freedom to mine the extensive resources of their library; Annetje and Nicky Louwerens of the staff of the Parapsychological Institute at the State University of Utrecht; and for advice, counsel, and extraordinary communications, Mrs. Mary Louise Suhm; Mr. William F. McCarthy, for carefully reading the typescript and suggesting numerous syntactical refinements.

Dozens of the leading parapsychologists in the world deplored the fact that Professor Tenhaeff's books have not been translated into English. Now that this one has been translated, it is earnestly to be hoped that means may be found to bring his nine other books to the English-speaking world. We have been too long in ignorance of what I believe may be of greater significance to the future of mankind than the power of the atom—the Power of Thought, as manifested in the revolutionary discoveries of parapsychology that smash time-space barriers. It might well be that Professor Tenhaeff's pioneering researches will someday be regarded in the same category as the discoveries of Copernicus, Freud and Einstein.

BERTHOLD ERIC SCHWARZ

PREFACE

Parapsychology has been defined as the branch of psychology devoted to the study of paranormal phenomena. These phenomena have been observed throughout the ages, which is understandable when we realize that they are rooted in general human capabilities.

Telepathy and clairvoyance in space and time, among other phenomena, belong in the paranormal class. They are elements of the collective concept called extra-sensory perception or paragnosis.

I have chosen to begin with the phenomenon of memory. From this starting point, I have set forth in the succeeding chapters a series of phenomena encountered in parapsychological research.

I want to express my gratitude to the translator and also to Berthold E. Schwarz, M.D. for their efforts toward publication of this little book in the English language.

The first edition appeared in 1957. Since then, it has been revised and reprinted several times, including a German version.

W. H. C. Tenhaeff

CONTENTS

Telepathy and
Clairvoyance

Chapter I

MEMORY

(to re-mind, or recollection)

Cryptomnesia

B<small>Y</small> *memory*, we mean the faculty or power of reproducing what we have experienced in the past. This power includes the ability to retain as well as to reproduce.

Besides the term memory, the psychologist also uses the term *recollection*, which has a broader meaning than memory. We speak of a recollection when that which is recalled is recognized *as such*.

If someone asks me in what year the Dutch Society for Psychical Research was established and who its first chairman was, I answer, "In 1920," and I mention Professor Heymans.

How do I know now that that year and the name which come to my mind are both correct?

G. E. Müller, who played such an important part in the development of the psychology of memory, pointed out that there are several distinguishing characteristics, or *correctness-criteria*, which cause the so-called awareness of correctness to develop. These correctness-criteria, which we can identify by introspection, are, first of all, the exclusiveness and the persistency with which this date and this name come up in my mind. Besides the prompt way in which this happens, there are also the clarity, vivacity, and what Müller calls the *Fülle*— the fullness or abundance of the ideas. By the term Fülle, Müller means that the images which well up in me are connected to others. In this example, the name "Heymans" did not arise by itself, but along with the year 1920; and I remember at the same time by association, among other things, that the constituting assembly was held in Amsterdam on April 1, 1920 and that Professor Heymans delivered an address on that occasion, *On the Purpose and Resources of a Society for Psychical Research,* which was published not long afterwards.

Finally, the recognition as such of what is recalled must be considered to be one of the correctness-criteria.

We know that the awareness of correctness which thus comes into being through the interplay of the various factors (correctness-criteria) is not always evenly strong. Nor is it always reliable, as the psychological testing of eyewitnesses has made plain.

Experience teaches us that we sometimes fail to recognize as such what is recalled. In these instances, negative memory disorders may develop. Charles Richet has named the phenomena based on negative memory disorders *cryptomnesic* (*kryptos* = hidden + *mnesis* = memory) phenomena.

When the phenomenon of cryptomnesia occurs in writers, the *unaware plagiarist* results. Many an author and composer has been guilty of this, Ed. Mörike among others. He wrote in *Mörike's Briefe, II*

> A short time ago, Uhland told me that he had found something in an old hand-written chronicle that compelled him to believe that I knew the Blaubeurer legend. In his opinion, I had made use of it when I wrote about a substance that made things invisible. I was quite astonished when I realized that my story coincided to such an extent with the legend. I could not remember ever having read this legend at all. And yet this must have been the case. . . .

Max Tak pointed out in *Radiobode* of July 24, 1931 that the musicologist as an unaware plagiarist is far from unknown. Tak wrote the following:

> I can completely and sympathetically agree with Dr. Elsa Bienenfeld, an Austrian musicologist who studied the problems of the conscious and unconscious plagiarist in the world of music and according to whom "there is no art so interspersed with conscious and unconscious borrowing."

Tak went on to say that it's an endless task to state even by approximation the number of unwitting little plagiarists.

Experience also teaches us that we absorb much more than we are aware of. Negative memory disorders or cryptomnesic phenomena can also arise from such source material. This is illustrated in the following case, reported by Freud in *The Interpretation of Dreams*. One of his patients dreamed that he ordered a small glass of *kontuszówka* in a café. The patient supposed that this beverage did not exist and that its very name was a figment of his imagination. Freud told him that on the contrary, kontuszówka was a Polish drink and that he must have seen it advertised on posters. At first the patient refused to believe it, but a couple of days later when he went to a café he paid more attention, looked at the posters, and sure enough, saw the name on an advertisement—and of all things, right on a street-corner he had passed at least twice a day for months.

That the parapsychologist needs to take the phenomenon of crypto-mnesia into account in his investigations can be learned from the following two cases. The first concerns a Mrs. B., who lived in the city of A. In July 1937 this lady received a postal money order. When she was ready to take it to the post office, however, the money order was nowhere to be found. Because she needed the money urgently, this "loss" placed her in a predicament. Again and again she asked herself where she could have left the money order. She herself had taken it from the letter box. She had put it aside so as to be able to present it as quickly as possible at the post office. All day long and that night she was bothered by the event, until she dreamed and saw the money order. In the morning upon awaking, however, she did not think of her dream until approximately 11 o'clock. Then, when a member of her household asked her if she had found the money order yet, she suddenly remembered her dream. She thereupon walked over to the buffet, pulled open a drawer, reached inside and triumphantly brought forth the money order! After doing this, she told the amazed household that in the dream she had seen it beneath the top side of the buffet, the drawers of which were crammed full of letters and notebooks. Now these drawers had been searched a couple of times, along with the rest of the house. Because the drawer was full, the money order had been shoved up between the slat and leaf when the drawer was opened. If she had taken the drawer completely out of the buffet, she would have found the money order quite a bit sooner.

To many this would seem an obvious case of clairvoyance. We can explain it much more simply, though, by assuming that, while pulling out the drawer, Mrs. B. glimpsed the money order stuck between the drawer contents and the top.

The following case is much more interesting. It concerns Hélène Smith, with whom we shall become more closely acquainted in Chapter V. One day during a séance, Hélène had a vision, in which an Arab appeared to her and held up a drawing before her. She picked up a pencil and a piece of paper, both conveniently at hand, and began to copy what she "saw" from left to right.

An investigation by Flournoy disclosed, contrary to his expectations, that the letters copied by Hélène were not only real Arabic script, but also formed the words *elqalil men alhabib ktsir*. They stood separate from one another, but together formed a proverb: "A little friendship means a lot." Although Hélène had never studied Arabic and had no knowledge of the letters, Flournoy suspected this to be a case of cryptomnesia and that therefore she must have seen this Arabic text somewhere in the past.

Further investigation revealed that her family physician, a Doctor Rapin, devoted his spare time to Oriental studies. When Professor Flournoy laid the text copied by Hélène before him, he exclaimed: "It is as if I see my own handwriting!" and proceeded to tell Flournoy that a number of years earlier he had taken a trip through North Africa and written an account of it. He had made gift copies of this travelog which he decorated with Arabic proverbs borrowed from a notebook which he used in studying Arabic. The first proverb in the notebook was the one copied by Hélène as occurring in her vision. The presumption was quite evident: she must once have had her hands on one of the gift copies. Doctor Rapin had distributed them, including, of course, the one in which he had written the above-mentioned proverb, among his friends and acquaintances. So her eye must have fallen on Doctor Rapin's handwritten words. This supposition gained in probability when we read in Flournoy's account that, as copied by Hélène, the text contained two errors in spelling. These mistakes did not show up in the notebook used by Doctor Rapin, but were probably made by him, because he published the travelog before he had fully mastered his Arabic.

The fact that the perfectly reliable and sincere Hélène was not only unable to remember having had the text under her eyes but was even quite serious in denying that she had ever had a copy of the description of the journey in her hands does not eliminate the supposition that, in a state of lowered consciousness, she had produced an eidetic image of the words written by Doctor Rapin in the itinerary, whereby the recognition of the material as such was lacking. For the results of investigations in regard to memory have not only shown that one can completely forget such facts, but also, as we have seen, that we take in much more than we are aware of.

Psychogenic Amnesia

In the second half of the 19th century, memory, along with many other psychological phenomena, became the subject of systematic experimental inquiry. In 1885 Ebbinghaus began his pioneer experiments, which were continued by G. E. Müller, Meumann, Binet and others.

Among the phenomena which were studied under experimental conditions was the *lasting mnemonic fixation*. This inquiry led to the observation that one can also forget the so-called permanently fixated. That is to say, one can also lose the ability to reproduce the fixated at will. We call this loss of power to reproduce the permanently fixated, "to *forget*."

According to the concept of classical psychology, forgetting exists as a fading away of dispositions and associations with the passage of time. This fading away is generally regarded as a normal process and as having nothing pathological about it.

Besides this normal nonpathological forgetfulness, there also exists a *pathological forgetfulness*—an abnormal forgetfulness. This brings us to the subject of *amnesia* (*a* = not + *mnesis* = memory).

Quite early, from experience with individuals suffering disorders and injuries of the cerebral cortex, we learned to recognize an abnormal kind of forgetfulness, requiring the attention of the neurologist.

Besides this, which is properly the concern of the neurologist, there is another type of pathological forgetfulness. Thanks to Freud and others, we know that there is a kind of forgetfulness of psychogenic origin which consequently becomes the concern of the psychologist and psychiatrist. This kind of forgetfulness is called *repression*.

Thus we recognize two kinds of amnesia, namely organic and

psychogenic. In what follows we shall be concerned only with the psychogenic kind.

As an example of psychogenic amnesia, I report the following case of a man who saw an arrested woman cleverly escape from the custody of two policemen by jumping over the parapet of a bridge. She drowned in full view of the onlookers. When interrogated soon afterwards about the way this incident had happened, this man, it appeared, could not remember several things which he certainly should have noticed. Later on, however, they returned to his memory. We call such a case, in which memory loss is related to impressions gained just after an emotional experience and which is of a transient nature, *regressive anterograde amnesia*.

We also encounter psychogenic amnesia in hypnotized persons, in whom we observe that upon awaking they have forgotten, in some cases at least, the conversation carried on with their doctor while under hypnosis.

Freud pointed out in *The Psychopathology of Everyday Life* that in our daily lives we all repeatedly exhibit amnesia. This is owing to the fact that we are inclined to repress unpleasant thoughts. Everyone has experienced an inability to get a name at a certain moment or the inability to remember where one has put a letter just received. If one takes notice in such instances of one's "thought-flashes," it will usually turn out that this name, this letter, etc. are associated with one or another unpleasant experience that one seeks to "forget" (suppress).

Hypermnesia

Prof. E. D. Wiersma mentions in his *Capita Psychopathologica*, Groningen, 1931, a 20-year-old female patient who became ill as a result of an assault on the street. A man accosted and threatened her. Consequently, she was severely frightened, and although afterwards she recounted the entire incident repeatedly—she could not even rid herself of the thought in the beginning—later on this picture disappeared so completely that she could not remember a thing about it. As a result of her fright from the assault, she suffered a nervous attack which was repeated every evening when she went to bed. As soon as she lay down, the attack would begin. She would raise herself up, open her eyes wide, and give the impression of being in a state of marked distress. She seemed to have hallucinations, warding off the attacker with her hands and crying out: "Go away, go away!" A few minutes later she would scream for help and make such a commotion that not only the household but also the neighbors were disturbed in their rest. These attacks regularly lasted for two or three hours, after which she would fall asleep. She would awaken on the following morning with a total amnesia concerning everything that had occurred during the night.

From this case it appears to us that, although in a waking state, this patient had lost all memory of the assault, its images had not disappeared. Under special circumstances—the hysterical fit—they recurred completely. In this condition, the patient was admitted to the clinic. Professor Wiersma himself attempted to establish contact with the patient by speaking to her while she slept, and also during an attack. In this, however, he did not succeed at all. But when he placed her under hypnosis, in a somnambulistic state, the fit did not occur, and he was thus certain of the cause of the attacks. Also, the patient was able to furnish the most accurate information about the assault.

This case is a clear example of *psychic* (so-called *hysterical*) *amnesia*[1]. The patient repressed what was for her too painful an experience, according to the analyst. While asleep or under hypnosis, both conditions of lowered consciousness, a weakening of the psychic inhibition—a diminution of the power of the censor (Freud)—occurs, and thus the amnesia is temporarily cancelled out. It can even happen that the balance swings to the other extreme, and the phenomenon of *hypermnesia* (*hyper* = stronger + *mnesis* = memory) appears. Instead of too little attention for the past, it becomes a focal point for too much attention. Here there exists differences of only a quantitative nature, and the one phenomenon can shift into the other.

Nevertheless, not only *repressed* experiences, knowledge, etc. can be recovered in states of lowered consciousness—in states in which inhibitions are weakened. Many instances are known of people who recall in their sleep what they try in vain to remember while awake. For example, we have this story from Dr. B. C. Goudsmit, former principal of a public high school at Zutfen.

After graduating from preparatory school at Leiden, I studied natural

sciences from 1865-1873. In 1874, eight years after I had last studied
Greek, I was visited at home by a student from the preparatory school
at Zutfen. The young man asked my help in translating the Greek verb
epataxe. I tried, but finally had to admit that I just could not come up
with it. But it bothered me all evening. My wife was present during
the conversation. The following day she asked me if I knew yet what
epataxe was. My negative answer made her laugh: 'How stupid, it is a
tense of the verb *tupto!*' What was obvious now? At night I had
dreamed aloud: '*tupto*—future *pataxo*—aorist *epataxe*, etc.' I completely forgot it the next morning. My wife, who does not know a word
of Greek, got up and wrote it down: *tupto, pataxo, epataxe.* It is obvious that I recovered in my dream memories from my prep school days,
which disappeared again on awaking.

Hypnotic Hypermnesia

By the term *hypnosis* we understand a state related to sleep charac-
terized, among other things, by a partial lowering of the consciousness level and also by a narrowing of the consciousness. The slackening of connections between ideas, which hypnosis shares with sleep,
causes a weakening of inhibitions. For that reason, the hypnotized
subject is often able to recall all sorts of long-forgotten, repressed
memories. It should, therefore, not surprise us that Freud initially
sought to bring his patients under hypnosis in order to make their
remembering easier.

One of the means employed by the hypnotist to bring his subject
or patient into a state of diminished inhibitions is the use of the so-
called *magic mirror,* of which several variations are known.

Dr. Justinus Kerner reports in his book, *Die Seherin von Prevorst*
("The Seeress of Prevorst"), that she had only to gaze at a soap bubble
to regain the memory of a dream, when she could not remember the
one she had the night before. Since we know that gazing at a re-
flecting surface has a hypnotic effect—can induce a lowered consciousness level—it should thus be evident that for the seeress, the
soap bubble functioned as a magic mirror. With its fragile aid she
could put herself into a condition in which inhibitions were diminished.

From its inception in 1882, the distinguished members of the British Society for Psychical Research took a special interest in the already
very ancient use of the magic mirror. Among these was Miss Good-

rich Freer, as reported in *Proceedings of the Society for Psychical Research,* Vol. V. Like the seeress from Prevorst, with the help of a magic mirror, she could put herself into a state in which inhibitions were diminished and in which hypnotic hypermnesia appeared. Instead of a soap bubble she used a crystal ball, as illustrated in the following case. Miss Freer wrote as follows:

> I had carelessly destroyed a letter without preserving the address of my correspondent. I knew the county, and searching on a map recognized the name of the town, one unfamiliar to me, but which I was sure I should know when I saw it. But I had no clue to the name of the house or street, till at last it struck me to test the value of the Crystal as a means of recalling forgotten knowledge. A very short inspection* supplied me with "H . . . . House" in gray letters on a white ground, and having nothing better to suggest from any other source, I risked posting my letter to the address so strangely supplied. A day or two later brought me an answer, headed "H . . . . House" in gray letters on a white ground.

As we have already seen, both forgotten and repressed memories arise in us under hypnosis. Now, since crystal gazing must be regarded as a classic method of achieving a condition of weakened inhibitions, it is a reasonable surmise that the magic mirror has also been utilized in psychoanalysis to help patients remember forgotten and repressed experiences. And this is indeed the case. In 1912 and 1913 the psychiatrist H. Silberer published several articles in *Zeitschrift für Psychoanalyse* ("Journal for Psychoanalysis") setting forth his use of the magic mirror. Other psychiatrists and psychologists have also done this.

In the fall of 1925 I undertook some tests with an unmarried nurse who was then about 40 years old. Among other things, I let her gaze into a crystal ball. On one occasion she told me that she saw in the ball a landscape of moonlit woods. In the foreground lay a giant upon whose stomach some gnomes were romping.

There can be no doubt at all that this was a daydream in which her desire for a husband and children was expressed. Another spinster, also about 40, saw a chain of wedding rings in the crystal ball.

---

* Staring into a crystal ball will cause a narrowing of the consciousness and a partial lowering of the level of consciousness, which brings the reporter into a state of autohypnosis.

It is certainly not too much to say that under certain conditions the magic mirror can be a valuable aid for the psychiatrist. It gives the patient, as it were, a chance to dream in his doctor's office and to inform the psychotherapist of the content of the dream. The magic mirror affords the medical man an opportunity to have recourse to hypnoanalysis; in this way, which need not be obvious, many patients can be analyzed with the aid of the crystal, completely unaware that they are under light hypnosis.

The Panoramic Life-Show

Let us direct our attention now to some cases of hypermnesia which are undoubtedly related to those already established in connection with hypnotized subjects.

The psychological phenomena which occur in cases of suddenly arising threats to life had already attracted the attention of psychologists in the second half of the 19th century. The famous French psychologist Th. Ribot noted in his book *Les maladies de la mémoire* ("Memory Disorders") (1881): "There are several stories in circulation regarding drowning persons who were saved from almost certain death at the last moment. All of their stories agree that at the very instant when they reached a state of apparent death, they saw in a single moment their entire lives, in the smallest detail, pass before them."

That this phenomenon was also known outside the circle of psychologists is evident from a treatise published by the noted Swiss geologist Prof. Albert Heim under the title *Notizen über den Tod durch Absturz* ("Notes on Death from Falls") (1891). He reported what several people who were about to perish during falls, but who escaped death by a lucky turn of events, had to say about their experiences. Heim concluded from his investigations that about 95 percent of persons meeting with accidents in the mountains have similar experiences. The extent of their intellectual development does not appear to influence these experiences.

According to Heim, most people who unexpectedly face death through an accident get the same psychic reaction. In this state they feel as follows:

> . . . no fear, no trace of despair, but rather a tranquil level-headedness,
> a complete surrender. . . Thoughts follow one another with tremendous

speed, thinking runs hundreds of times faster than under normal circumstances. . . In numerous cases, persons meeting with an accident gain a sudden retrospective view of their entire past. . . .

It is significant that Heim himself also underwent this experience on one occasion. During a climb in the Sanctis Range in the spring of 1871, he slipped and suffered a fall which could have cost him his life. According to Heim, the fall lasted perhaps 15 or at the most 25 seconds. In that brief time, an extraordinarily large number of thoughts went through his head. He had pseudo-hallucinations, and relived his childhood and adolescence. One second during his fall was equal in his "feeling" to five minutes. Like a number of other people who were faced with an accident, Heim also experienced additional phenomena.[2]

In September 1937 I delivered a series of radio talks on parapsychological subjects. Among other things, on this occasion I covered "shock thinking" and asked those among my listeners who had undergone such experiences to report them to me. Several dozen people replied, including Mrs. D. H.-A., who wrote:

> With reference to your request, I can tell you that both times I courted danger, I very clearly saw my life unroll before my spiritual eye like a kind of film. The exact duration is hard for me to fix, but I think that everything was unreeled within a few minutes.
>
> It happened the first time 15 years ago. I was running the vacuum-cleaner, when suddenly the electric current went through me. At first it seemed as if my head was spinning round and round. After that, it seemed as if I could think very clearly. All sorts of things which had made an impression on me came up. First, images of my childhood years. I saw myself sitting on the wheel of a street-organ with a doll in my arms which I rocked in time to the music. I saw my father going to a funeral in his Sunday best and a high silk hat (I would then have been about three years old). Further scenes from my school years, my engagement, my marriage. I saw the birth of my sons. All kinds of pictures from those years came back to me. When I came to, I thought, 'That would have been a beautiful death. To die, with so many and such clear images before one's eyes is not so bad.'
>
> At first I supposed that it had been the electric current which caused my lucidity of spirit. But four years later, while canoeing with my son, I fell overboard, and because of my heavy clothing sank and had a hard time coming up again. I saw my life movie for the second time. Now I understood that it had nothing to do with electricity. This time I also saw my deceased husband on his death-bed and heard his last words.

Some other scenes from our marriage appeared to me as well. The main thought concerned Ferdie, my youngest son, who fell into the water with me. I suspect that all of this lasted less than a minute. As soon as I was above water and saw the face of my son and our capsized boat, the struggle for our lives was on, and all the memories vanished.

After we felt solid ground under our feet and set about making the boat navigable, I asked my son if anything special had happened to him while he was under water. "Nothing, Mother, I only thought of you and how I could help you." For a long time after this happened, I had trouble getting rid of various images. . . .

One of the questions that arise when reading these and similar reports of "shock thinking" is whether one really sees the *entire* past moving by, or only a few moments out of it. Possibly we are dealing here with an exaggeration, all the more so because of the number of "hallucinations" which seem to follow one after another.

V. Egger was among the first to discuss the illusion of the life-panorama. In two essays published in *Revue Philosophique* ("Philosophical Review") in 1896, he considered an "unrolling" of the entire life-panorama to be out of the question. He believed that only a few scenes are involved, and that it is later on that one supposes inaccurately that one saw one's entire past move by.

The same opinion seems to have been held by the Swiss theologian and psychoanalyst Oskar Pfister. In his treatise *Schockdenken und Schockfantasien bei höchster Todesgefahr* ("Shock-thinking and fantasies in deadly peril") (1931), he wrote that it would be impossible to give an accurate account of such an incident, it being said that one sees at a critical moment, in a few seconds, one's whole life filing past. According to Pfister, "Nur um eine kleine Auslese kann es sich handeln" ("It can only be a question of a small selection") there can only be, so to speak, a few instances. He then went on to pose the question—and in this he went beyond Egger—: According to what principle of selection is the choice made?

An accidental encounter with a 45-year-old war veteran presented Pfister with a valuable contribution towards an answer to this question. Thirteen years earlier, this man had found himself in deadly peril in the trenches. An exploding shell killed all of his comrades-in-arms in the immediate vicinity. He himself remained miraculously unharmed. He nevertheless fell to the ground with a thud, and for a moment thought he was badly wounded and dying. At that moment he saw his "entire life" pass by.

Pfister then asked his informant—who felt his experience should be subjected to a psychoanalytical examination—to tell him everything. What precisely did he remember about the moment when the shell exploded and he thought he was dying? What did he see passing before his spiritual eye? It turned out that a total of only four image groups were involved, all laden with emotional content. These were now subjected one by one to a psychoanalytical examination by Pfister. This inquiry led him to conclude that those who claimed to see their whole life passing by during one or another accident were victims of an illusion. In reality, Pfister claimed, they saw only a few moments out of all this. As a result of the psychoanalytical examination, Pfister claimed to understand just why only these and no other moments came up out of the past. The fragmentary life-show and the shock-fantasies serve a purpose, according to Pfister. They conjure before our eyes, he claimed, a beautiful reality, so that we won't see the unbearable one.

Egger's first essay in *Revue Philosophique* caused several of his readers to reach for a pen. Doctor Sollier was one of them. He correctly pointed out that life-panoramas, whether fragmentary or not, were not reported only by persons who almost lost their lives through accidents. Informants included also men and women who claimed to have seen their past, whether fragmentary or not, rushing by from their sickbed. One of these he reported was a young woman who experienced great peril three times in her life. The first time, at age 17, she suffered from typhus. She overheard the doctors, who were sure she was dying, say it was only a matter of a few hours. The thought that she was dying caused no particular reaction in her. The second time (she was then under treatment by Sollier) it happened when she suffered an internal hemorrhage after a confinement. She got the impression she was dying. Her thoughts were not directed at the past, but at the future of those whom she loved and would have to leave behind. The third time she was in great danger caused by appendicitis complicated by peritonitis, and she experienced the phenomenon of the life-panorama. She told Sollier, who also treated her on that occasion, that she saw her past life—from her youth onwards—roll by in chronological order.[3] The images flowed slowly past her. Sollier speaks here about an *"inventaire de son moi"* ("inventory of her self").

I found an analogous case in the *Journal of the American Society for Psychical Research* (1931). It concerned an experience of Leslie Grant Scott in Ceylon. She wrote the following:

> Dying is really not such a terrifying experience. It is quite easy, quite simple in fact. Birth, I imagine, is far more awful. I speak as one who has died and come back, and who found Death one of the easiest things in life—but not the returning. That was difficult and full of fear.
>
> The circumstances surrounding and leading up to Death are often painful and terrible, but they have nothing to do with Death itself. Rather do they belong to Life, and are often present when dying does not result.
>
> I was in bed, a large, old fashioned bed in which I seemed lost. A friend was sitting beside me. I lay there quietly thinking and feeling more at peace than I had felt for some time. Suddenly my whole life began to unroll before me and I saw the purpose of it. All bitterness was wiped out for I knew the meaning of every event and I saw its place in the pattern. I seemed to view it all impersonally but yet with intense interest and although much that was crystal clear to me then, has again become somewhat veiled in shadow, I have never forgotten or lost the sense of essential justice and rightness of things.

She went on to write that she became suddenly aware that she was dying and announced this to her visitor, who immediately sent for the doctor, Sir Aldo Castellani. He diagnosed the condition of his patient as critical, and his immediate intervention succeeded in bringing her back to earthly existence.

The fact which is deserving of our attention, and which the informant noticed, was that this life-panorama seemed to have a *goal.* Particularly so, because other reporters have also shown us that there is a possibility that the life-show has a teleological meaning. I am thinking here, for instance, of what we have read by Léon Chapot on the Venerable Mother Marie de l'Incarnation. On the day of her conversion,[4] she was supposed to have experienced a life-panorama, whether fragmentary or not, in which, primarily, her mistakes and shortcomings were deeply accentuated. M. Perty reports a similar case. It concerned von Uexküll, who wrote him a letter on May

23, 1869 telling him about a repeating dream. This "dream" was repeated three nights in a row, and he seemed to see his whole life "von frühester Kindheit bis zur Gegenwart" ("from earliest childhood to the very present") pass by with an uncommon clarity. The meaning of this dream was obvious to von Uexküll—to elevate and to purify him.

We find the teleological significance of the life-panorama described further in the writings of theosophist authors (C. W. Leadbeater, A. Besant, M. Heindel and others), according to whom Man after death sees his entire life in retrospect (with the meaning that he renders an accounting). Heindel writes the following:

> When Man is released from his physical body, the total of his spent life runs like a panorama before him, but the incidents follow one another in reverse order. The occurrences of the days immediately before his death come back first and go through adulthood, youth, childhood and infancy. Everything crops up out of the remembrance. Man stands as an onlooker before the panorama of his spent life. He sees scenes gliding past . . . This panorama lasts from a few hours up to a few days. . . This curious outline of life after death corresponds with what happens when somebody drowns or falls from a great height.[5] In such instances Man sees his whole life in a flash, because he loses consciousness instantly.

Although I am unwilling to accept what we read in the books of the theosophist authors without more evidence, it is my opinion, however, that some of their assertions have a certain heuristic[6] value and can serve as a guide. Furthermore, many of their ideas concerning the life-panorama are in agreement with the reports of our informants. In my opinion, though, we cannot conclude from the above that Egger and Pfister are mistaken. They rightly call into question several statements of correspondents regarding the life-panorama and believe that these reporters are unconsciously guilty of overestimating the number of images viewed. Our criticism relates only to their apodictic contention that there are never more than a small number of scenes. The data furnished by Sollier and others give us ample basis for doubting their apodictic statement, for they maintain an unwarranted generalization.

Furthermore, there are the experiences which we obtain from psychoscopists. They afford us an opportunity to speak out and to suggest that Egger and his followers dismiss the subject much too easily. For have we not observed, in frequently repeated experiments with paragnosts, that they come into contact with those who consult them by such paranormal means as telepathy and mind reading? All sorts of more or less fragmentary images—often more or less forgotten—out of the past of those seeking advice pass before the spiritual eye[7] of the paragnost. It seems as if, in a number of cases, fragments of the life-panorama of their consultants are "seen" by the psychoscopists.

Such more or less fragmentary "inspection" of the past of their consultants (*retroscopy*) would most likely not be possible if these consultants in principle were not able to recall their past life in the smallest details. Although I shall cover this matter more thoroughly in Chapter II, I believe that this section should not be concluded without an illustration of this kind. Therefore I have borrowed a few experiences of the notable Swiss (liberal) politician and pedagog, Heinrich Zschokke, from his autobiography *Eine Selbstschau,* Aarau, 1843.

Without at first being aware of them, he had at his disposal remarkable paragnostic gifts. Zschokke wrote the following:

> When I met a stranger for the first time, it sometimes happened that when I listened silently to his talk, his past with numerous little details would be revealed to me. The way in which this was disclosed to me was suggestive of a dream, but was, however, clear to me. Usually, the things mentioned lasted for only a few minutes. But in that short length of time, as a rule, I became so completely absorbed in them that finally I neither saw the face of the speaker nor heard his voice any more.[8] This phenomenon occurred to me spontaneously.
>
> For a long while, I considered these fleeting visions as products of the playful capers of my fantasy, the more so because these visions showed me the clothing, movements of the person in question, the room, household articles, and other accessory matters of minor importance. Once, only as a joke and strictly confidentially, I told Kirschberg and his family the secret story of a sewing woman. Being in the family circle gave me confidence. The seamstress had just left the room and the house. I had never seen her before. They began laughing as I told the story. I was asked how I could have gotten all this. When I told those present that she was a total stranger to me and that nobody had ever told me anything about her, they refused to believe me. I myself was no less amazed than the others present at the fact that my visions

(dream-images) coincided with reality. From then on I paid more attention, and when the occasion called for it and I was permitted to do so, I took the opportunity. I would then narrate to those whose life glided past my spiritual eye the contents of my vision, to provoke either denial or confirmation. While I always got a confirmation, those who gave it to me were always baffled by what I seemed to know. . . .

On a market-day, arriving in the city of Waldshut, I put up at an inn called "Zum Rebstock." In the evening, we ate at a table occupied to full capacity. . . .

Zschokke went on to relate how the conversation accidentally veered towards clairvoyance and related phenomena. A young man who sat opposite him began to ridicule this in the most exuberant manner.

. . . The life of this young man began right then to glide past me. I asked him if he would be honest enough to concur if I, who had only just met him for the first time, related an event out of his past which he was anxious to keep secret. He openly promised that he would confirm whatever I said if I spoke the truth. Whereupon I told him what my vision showed. The entire company learned the history of the young merchant: his student years, his minor escapades, finally a small sin he had committed against his employer; he had taken some cash. I described, further, the unoccupied room with white-painted furniture: to the right was a door, painted brown, and to the left there stood on a table a small black cash-box. . . During this narrative a dead silence hung over the company. From time to time I broke the silence by asking if I spoke the truth. The startled young man confirmed everything I said. . . Touched by his straightforwardness, I extended my hand to him. . . .

Bergson's Speculations about the Function of the Brain

Some very interesting cases of partial hypermnesia can be observed among the mentally deficient. In the year 1925 at the psychology laboratory of the State University at Utrecht I had under observation a blind imbecile whose memory had a noteworthy capacity for dates and music.[9]

The French philosopher H. Bergson seeks to explain remarkable performances of this kind through his speculations (also of great value to anatomists and physiologists)[10] about the inhibiting function of the brain.

Bergson concludes that thinking (consciousness) cannot be a function of the brain, as the materialistic energetic monists imply, and also, that those thinkers (idealistic monists) who view the brain only as a mode of appearance of consciousness likewise find themselves on the wrong track. According to him, an exponent of dualism, one may only say that consciousness is "hung up" on the brain. With Plato, he tends to see the body only as an organic means to act in the world, and to a certain extent to consider it as our "grave."

Bergson claims we may consider the brain only as an organ to give us an opportunity to focus our attention on this earthly life. It prevents us from obtaining knowledge which is not relevant to our earthly existence. But as soon as morbid conditions develop, he says, the door which until now was closed is "set ajar." Here Bergson voices a thought with which we are already familiar in Kant.[11] The light shed by parapsychological research justifies this idea. In other words, Bergson seems to have recognized that under certain conditions, morbid disorders must be regarded as favorable circumstances for the manifestation of hitherto latent knowledge acquired in a paranormal way.

The brain canalizes and also limits the life of the mind, Bergson told the members of the Society for Psychical Research in London on May 28, 1913. It prevents us from turning our eyes to right and left and it prevents us also as far as possible from turning to look back. We may devote our attention to the past only to the extent that the past can serve us, to prepare for the future or to throw light on it. Under abnormal conditions it can happen, however, that our brain can no longer "mask" the past.

A great many people who have experienced extreme danger, as we have seen, have told us that, at those moments which they fancied to be their last, they saw their whole past filing by. According to Bergson, the origin in fact for the phenomenon of the panoramic vision of the totality of past life is found at the instant that we face death because we then begin to lose our interest in this earthly existence (*notre attention à la vie*). The door, till now closed, begins to open (is "set ajar") with the result that we direct our attention more than normally to the past. (In other words: the significance of the phenomenon classified as hypermnesic panoramic vision of the life-show depends, according to Bergson, on a debilitation of the inhibitory mechanism, as a result of which we lose interest in our earthly existence.)

Bergson claims this is the way we should explain the supernormal memory feats of the mentally retarded and other deficients. His view would ascribe them to the fact that these people possess brains that are not fully developed, and such brains are incapable of fulfilling the inhibitory task of allowing them to forget in an appropriate manner.

Chapter II

TELEPATHY

(recollection and "inneren" *)

The Psychoscopists

Parapsychological research brings us into contact with persons known heretofore as psychometrists. I personally prefer to call them psychoscopists, as I regard the term psychometry as ill-chosen. Psychometry was first applied in 1842 by J. R. Buchanan.

By *psychoscopist*, I mean a paragnost who commonly makes use of an object (a so-called *inductor*) as an aid.

The concept of *paragnosis* (or extrasensory perception) is a collective one, comprised of *telepathy* and *clairvoyance* in space and time as its most important elements. Clairvoyance in time can be divided into clairvoyance in the past, in the present, and in the future. Clairvoyance in space must be considered as synonymous with clairvoyance in the present.

Those of us who have experimented with psychoscopists know that in great part, their abilities can be traced to telepathy and mind reading.[1]

The following illustration will serve as an example of a psychoscopic experiment in which the results obviously depend on telepathy (or possibly on mind reading). It concerns Mrs. L. M., with whom I conducted tests[2] as early as 1929. On July 6, 1929 I handed her an envelope containing a passport belonging to Mr. K., whom I personally knew very well. She put her right hand part way into the partially opened envelope. She made no effort to look at the

---

* *Inneren*: Things, ideas, concepts, events, places, etc., coming up in one's mind without previous experience, as if welling up out of an inner spring. Since there is no English word with this meaning, we use "inneren" set off by quotation marks. —Translator

picture, which was to serve as an inductor but which contained no clues for practical purposes. And then Mrs. M. commented as follows:

> Someone who reads and writes a lot. He is at home in any field. He performs journalistic work. He is quickly stimulated. He leads a hurried and irregular life. I see him writing while seated in a train. He picks up every scrap of news. This is not just curiosity, he has to keep abreast of everything that happens. He can be very curt at times. Stacks of paper lie on his desk. There is an infernal disorder. He has a sense of humor. He speaks foreign languages. Machines form part of his environment. I hear a regular thumping sound. The air reeks there. I smell a peculiar, vile scent. The uproar there is awful. He himself does not work among these machines, but he walks between them. He sits as a desk. He has a feeling for poetry. He gets a lot of books sent to him.

When we know what was totally unknown to Mrs. M., that in those days Mr. K. was the managing editor of a provincial newspaper, then we must allow that in this case we are faced with a direct hit. I was in frequent touch with Mr. K. in those days. I visited his office several times, and there was ordinarily an "infernal disorder." From time to time during our talks, he'd stroll into the composing room to give various instructions. It smelled of printer's ink, and there were the noises familiar to every visitor to a printing plant. Mr. K. was always after the latest news, traveled a lot by train in those days, possessed a good sense of humor, was a lover of poetry, and sometimes gave me books which he had received for review.

Recollection and "Inneren"

Considering all of this, we are led to suppose that Mrs. M. was able to pick up in her mind the thoughts that could cross mine when I saw the passport photo. In other words, when touching the portrait she had the power to bring into her mind what I was able to remember when seeing the picture.

With this, we arrive at the essence of telepathy. Telepathy, then, is the receipt in one's mind of thoughts that emanate from the consciousness of another person. It must be pointed out that the picture was no more of a prerequisite for my remembering all sorts of things about Mr. K. than, as an inductor, it seemed indispensable to the psychoscopist's "inneren." Experience has taught us that a number of psychoscopists seem able to pick up other people's thoughts without the use of an inductor.

From the statements of various psychoscopists who have been tested and questioned about their introspections, it is evident that they seem inclined also to equate their telepathic performances with feats of memory. The following account in *Algemeen Handelsblad* (Dec. 23, 1933) was reported by Mr. F. van Raalte, who for years served this Amsterdam newspaper as education editor. It concerns a social worker with whom he came in contact through correspondence.

The social worker wrote the following to Mr. van Raalte:

> There was a small boy of about nine from Zaandam, who came in with both of his parents. The little fellow sat opposite me and answered my questions properly until all at once he broke down. I then grabbed his left hand without quite realizing why I did it² and saw in my imagination—*as though I had seen it before and just now remembered*—the little boy enter the front door of his home, lift the slot of the letter-box and remove a square, light gray envelope. Next, I saw in my memory— that is to say, it could not be memory because this was the first time I had seen this boy and I had never been in Zaandam, *but the way this happened, seeing inwardly, could be compared to remembering*—the boy went into a hall. To do this he had to pass through a glass half-door which swung both ways on a spring-hinge. Then he walked through another doorway. I could not see what was beyond that door, but I suspected it was the bathroom. Then I saw that I was right. The boy threw the letter which he had taken from the box into the toilet and went back into the hallway. That was all I saw.
>
> So then I told the boy that he had taken the letter out of the letter-box and thrown it into the toilet and that I wanted him to tell me who had sent that letter. Crying, the boy claimed he didn't know. But I told him that he knew very well, as otherwise he would have had no reason to get rid of it. I even insisted that he must have known what was in the letter. Still weeping, the boy claimed that truly he didn't know— hadn't he thrown the unopened letter into the toilet? He then had to hear that this information made an established case of it. He had purloined a letter addressed to his father, and he was expected to supply, if not its text, then at least the subject covered in the letter. After some deliberation, the boy saw that he could no longer maintain his 'I don't know' and then, finally, came the confession: he had taken something, ' I don't remember what' out of his teacher's bag at school.
>
> Knowing that this information had never been in my mind before, I

had to accept as a fact that it entered my mind when I took the boy
by his hand.

Having become interested in the telepathic (psychoscopic) powers
of his correspondent, Mr. van Raalte at once asked him to permit
him to witness such an event. Because they did not live very far
away from each other, he witnessed similar questionings several times
without, however, experiencing anything unusual.

Mr. van Raalte said the following:

Everything followed the normal course of events at the children's
and adolescent's police court and the Youth Foundation, and we had
about decided not to waste any more time listening in on similar, tire-
some hearings, which always covered the same kind of childhood misdeeds. When yet another invitation came, we decided that this would
be the last time we'd go. But this time something did happen. The
delinquent was a slender sixteen-year-old girl from a good family. Your
reporter sat in a corner of the room, writing. The girl and her aunts,
who accompanied her, could see him half-hidden behind a stack of
books on the desk. This was done so that his presence would not be
disturbing to the expected confession.

The confessions came up very smoothly: a quarter taken from an aunt's
change purse, another quarter, then a guilder that lay on a table and a
maid was accused of the theft—this also happens so often when children
take money—and then it seemed as if the stream of confessions was
dammed up. The girl became silent and her face showed that she was
trying her utmost to remember some more crimes. The interrogator
sympathetically encouraged her: "Come on, tell us some more, it doesn't
make the case any worse, but better; don't suppress anything, one time
more or less does not mean a thing." [4] Suddenly he took hold of her
left hand with his left hand and said, while he closed his eyes: "I see
you standing in a kitchen, by a glass cupboard. You open a little door
and remove a small basket made of brown reed—I mean they call it
wicker. The inside of that basket is lined with colored material, it's
called upholstery or cottage material, something like that. I see lots of
black with little colored flowers, and the basket has a high handle, bent
of brown reed, smooth reed. There are silver coins in that basket, big
guilders and rijksdollars, and I see that you are taking some of them
out. The truth—how many did you take?"

The two aunts nodded to confirm that the "seer" saw correctly and
the young girl admitted it—she had taken money from the little basket,
four guilders.

Later we witnessed another similar case. The interrogator saw "in
thought" a boy on vacation at The Hague with a shopping basket on
his arm, scribbling with a pencil on a scrap of paper. The boy admitted

that it was a falsified account of the money he had paid in a store, so
that he could withhold a guilder. The interrogator and the boy were in
Amsterdam when he "saw" what the boy had done at The Hague.
This time also, he took the boy's left hand with his left hand. . . .

Another paragnost, Stephan Ossowiecki,[5] who repeatedly succeeded
in obtaining impressions of the contents of sealed envelopes containing drawings or written sheets of paper, replied to an investigator's
question as to what the connecting link in his introspections was that
the inductor was only an aid and as such not absolutely necessary.
This aid only helped him "to attain telepathic contact" with who-
ever had written on the paper, and it would make no difference
whether or not the writer were present at the sitting. Ossowiecki
said the following:

> At a certain moment, I get the feeling that I am the person who wrote
> the words on that paper or who made the drawings on it, and then what
> he thought, the sentences he wrote, spring up in my mind like a memory.
> It is as if I remember all this. What he has thought, I see again before
> me. The important thing is for me to attain telepathic contact with this
> person. If I don't succeed, then nothing happens. I don't always achieve
> an easy telepathic relationship with all people. With some it comes
> quite easily, but there are also those with whom I have no luck . . .

The behavior of psychoscopists during their sittings is entirely consistent with these statements. Those of us who have observed them
know that their behavior often suggests that they are searching for
a word, a name, or an event. We all know from experience that
when we search for a name that has escaped us, sometimes a name
will come up which is associated with the forgotten one. It can also
happen that a fragment of a so-called forgotten name emerges (*step-
by-step apperception.*)

Now, something similar is observable in psychoscopists. In my
published articles, I have frequently given examples of the emerging
of associated images. Here is still another one. It concerns Mr. Beta.
One day, under my supervision in a group of several dozen people
entirely unknown to him, he "manipulated" a number of objects or
inductors. In his absence, these objects had been laid on a small
table, from which he took one after another for handling. At one
particular moment, he took a car key from the table. After a
moment's silence, Mr. Beta said:

An image of a little school-book that I read as a boy in school comes to me. There is a story, it made a deep impression on me at the time. A church on fire, a boy* rushed into this burning church to save the monstrance. Monstrance, monstrance. What does this gentleman have to do with a monstrance?

When the question remained unanswered, the paragnost followed with: "Now I have to think about my nephew Frans. He was always called *Onze Frans* (our Frans). Monstrance... Our Frans... What could this mean? It is a name? Does this little key belong to somebody named Monfrans or Montfrans?" The owner of the key was named Montfrans.

Encouraged by this success, which strengthened his self-confidence, the subject then began to report "impressions" which were correct, but not relevant to this illustration.

The following is a poignant example of the emerging of associated images in a paragnost. It concerns one with whom I experimented in telepathy. Sitting in a room separate from the subject, I drew a sketch of a windmill. After the experiment, the subject showed me a piece of paper on which he had written the name Pentinga. When I asked him what made him think of this name, he replied that he had spent his youth in a village in Friesland, and that the name of the miller in that village was Pentinga.

Th. Besterman reported a fine example of step-by-step apperception in an account of a test performed with the previously mentioned Stephan Ossowiecki in Warsaw in 1933. An opaque closed envelope, sealed in London, served as an inductor. This envelope contained two other envelopes, likewise opaque, bearing distinguishing marks. The third envelope contained a piece of paper, folded double, on which Mr. Besterman had drawn an ink bottle. To the left of the bottle he had written the word "Swan" and to the right "Ink" in block letters.

On September 29, 1933 this inductor was given to Ossowiecki in Warsaw by Lord Charles Hope. Lord Hope was in ignorance as to the contents of the envelope, and it should be noted also that Mr. Besterman remained in London. After the paragnost had obtained

---

* When I asked Mr. Beta about this boy he told me that as a schoolboy he felt inclined to identify himself with the hero of this story.

some impressions regarding Mr. Besterman, he began to describe the contents of the sealed envelope. He "saw" both of the other envelopes and then got fragmentary impressions of the drawing, which he sketched. It is apparent from the reproduction of Ossowiecki's three sketches that the total impression was built-up step-by-step from its elements. Finally, the subject drew a bottle with the word "Swan" on the left and the word "Ink" on the right. When the subject declared that the experiment was over, the envelopes (after a check to see that the seals were undamaged) were opened. The final drawing made by the subject appeared to conform quite well with that prepared by Mr. Besterman in London.

This case is most readily explained by the subject having attained a telepathic relationship with Mr. Besterman. In a paranormal way (telepathy or thought reading) he borrowed from Mr. Besterman's psyche his knowledge of the contents of the sealed envelopes.

When we listen attentively to the words that psychoscopists use, it becomes apparent that their impressions are forced upon them. Often these forced impressions pass into pseudo-hallucinations. Occasionally, these pseudo-hallucinations shade off into hallucinations.[6]

That the pseudo-hallucinations of paragnosts are not limited to sight alone should already be evident from the example of Mrs. M., who not only saw Mr. K. seated in his office, but also "heard" the thumping of the printing presses and furthermore sensed the "smell" of printer's ink in her nose.

Here again we can draw a parallel with what happens while remembering.

Differential psychology, which studies the individual differences regarding quantitative relations, has shown, among other things, that people differ from one another in the vividness and clarity of their recalls. Galton had already pointed out in 1880 that when a large number of people are asked how clearly they can imagine the things they see everyday at the breakfast table, one gets the most divergent answers. At one extreme are those who claim to be able to see these objects in memory almost as clearly as when they actually saw them, and at the other there are those who say they know how these objects looked to them but are unable to imagine graphically how they look. In between is a large middle group of people in gradations from the two extremes.

As Urbantschitsch, Jaensch and others have shown, the faculty of visualizing is present in some people to such an extent as to warrant placing them in a special category. With this we approach the subject of *eidetic images.*[7]

As we saw earlier in Chapter I, it seems that because of the diminution of inhibitions, people under hypnosis can remember many different events of which they have lost all memory in the waking state. When, as in many cases, forgotten memories appear to be suppressed remembrances, they can as such often cause the development of a variety of neurotic disorders. And so it turned out that the discovery of hypnotic hypermnesia, which has contributed in an important degree to the development of psychoanalytical treatment, has a therapeutic value. Freud initially used hypnosis to restore in his patients consciousness of various suppressed memories.

Not only hypnosis, but also so-called automatic writing is of value in psychotherapy.

By *automatic writing* we mean in psychology a phenomenon which can be observed in quite a number of people. It consists in the fact that, with paper at their disposal, they pick up a pencil and begin to write automatically (that is to say, without the intervention of their conscious will). While writing automatically, the subject or patient can carry on a conversation with the experimenter or doctor, or read a book. The writing "happens by itself," and usually the subject feels as if a power outside himself makes use of his hand.

As for the content of what is written, this seems in a number of cases to have had a connection with events which occurred in the subject's past but which he cannot consciously remember. In such cases, it is as if, behind the personality of the subject, there is a second personality possessing a more complete knowledge of the subject's past than he himself has. It also seems as if this "second being"[8] is sometimes in a position to answer all sorts of questions the experimenter may ask about the past of the subject.

It should not be assumed that the content of automatically written communications is limited to the past of the subject and is therefore only of psychoanalytical value.[9] Pioneers in parapsychological research have already established that the sensualistic dogma (according to which nothing can be in our minds that has not previously reached us through our senses) cannot be sustained because of the content of a number of automatically written communications. For haven't various so-called mediums been able to prove their paragnostic gifts by automatically written messages? (That, through ignorance of the phenomenon already reported of the dramatic splitting up of the personality, these "mediums" are often led to accept a spiritistic explanation need not concern us here.) Here I am thinking, for example, of William Stainton Moses,[10] who could learn the contents of closed books by paranormal means (book-tests), as was apparent from some of his automatically produced messages.

As a well-known variant of automatic writing, I will mention first planchette writing. The *planchette* consists of a small piece of wood mounted on three casters and provided with a pencil holder. A pencil can be inserted into this so as to mark a piece of paper if one moves the planchette over it on a table. One of the advantages that the planchette has over an ordinary pencil is that it moves very easily, and letters can be written by its use without the person, who unconsciously moves it, being aware of their character. A second advantage of the planchette over a pencil, I think, is that more than one person can make use of it at the same time. It thus forms a transition to the so-called Ouija Board.

By *Ouija Board* (from the French *oui* and German *ja*) we mean a piece of paper, usually glued to cardboard, provided with the letters of the alphabet. Usually, also, the board has the numbers from 0 to 9, in addition to the words "Yes," "No," "Maybe" and "Stop." Besides this, the board is furnished with a moveable cross, consisting of two crossed slats with a wooden pointer attached at the crossing point. Four people hold the ends of the cross loosely. When the subjects are correctly chosen, it will be found that after a little while the cross begins to move (a movement originated by automatic movements of the sitters), and the pointer begins to tap the letters, thus forming words and sentences.

As can be expected, the content of messages obtained by means of the planchette, the Ouija Board and other related "instruments"[11] can be identified in many cases as forgotten or suppressed memories. Also, all sorts of wishes, whether suppressed or not, can be revealed in this manner. This does not minimize in any way the help one can get from these devices under certain circumstances for possibly getting messages which testify to the telepathic receptivity (paragnostic powers) of the "mediums" (subjects). In Chapter VII of my book *Het Spiritisme*, the case is cited of a 15-year-old schoolboy in Vlissingen, who without being aware of it, telepathically influenced one of the participants in a spiritistic seance. The Ouija Board was being used. The result was that the pointer spelled out letters which together formed the (mutilated) text of a short poem in English which the boy, whose thoughts went out continuously to the circle, was reading in his home at the time. The house in which the seance was held was situated at quite some distance from the one in which the boy lived.

Another similar case is described in the same book. Instead of the Ouija Board, the members of the circle used a table—so-called *Table-tipping*—which, like the Ouija Board, and also based on the so-called ideomotor principle, began to move and spell out words.

Those who have experimented with psychoscopists know that several of them produce sensory as well as motor automatisms. I think here, for example, of Mr. Beta, a paragnost who worked as a private detective and in that capacity was successful more than once in furnishing useful data in cases of missing persons or thefts. I repeatedly saw him write down words and names automatically at the start of a consultation, and also make sketches of the terrain in connection with the case about which he was being consulted. Afterwards, he would usually put the pencil aside and then his impressions came in the form of "inspirations" and pseudo-hallucinations.

On several occasions another psychoscopist, Mr. Zeta, employed a divining rod during consultations. The movements of the rod are also based on the ideomotor principle. . . .

If we review all that we have covered so far, we must acknowledge that we have accumulated quite a few arguments favoring the assumption that, in telepathy, we are dealing with "inneren". We can, however, adduce still more arguments in support of this thesis.

It was shown earlier in Chapter I that in studying our faculty of memory we recognize the awareness of correctness. It occurs through the interplay of several factors—the so-called correctness criteria—but it doesn't always seem to be evenly strong. Also, psychological testing of eye witnesses has disclosed that the awareness of correctness is not always reliable.

The pressing question is this: Can we again encounter, through research in telepathy and related phenomena, this awareness of correctness? Those who have observed paragnosts are certain that this is indeed the case. It has struck me again and again, during my experiments with psychoscopists, that the knowledge which forces itself on them through paranormal means often goes hand in hand with an awareness of correctness.

Especially in open meetings, where some among those present quite often seem to derive a certain amount of pleasure from maintaining a reserved attitude towards the subject, I have often had the opportunity to ascertain that the awareness of correctness can not only be counted on to be forceful, but also often seems to be reliable. To illustrate this, let's take two random examples.

On the occasion of a meeting of some members of the Dutch Society for Psychical Research, the psychoscopist, Mr. Alpha, handled a closed envelope. He remarked that obviously it contained a letter requesting money for the purchase of a mantelpiece. After the psychoscopist had reported his impressions, the lady who had laid the letter on the table told him that what he had said about the mantelpiece was incorrect. Mr. Alpha retorted that he was sure that what he had said was in the letter. Wherewith, obtaining the consent of the lady, he handed me the letter with the request that I read it. Indeed, there was something written about a request for money in connection with the purchase of a mantelpiece.

It remains for us to surmise that the lady who supplied the letter as an inductor had been unpleasantly touched by this request. She suppressed the knowledge. This suppression of an idea, which obviously was brought on by a strong feeling of uneasiness, no doubt promoted this telepathic transference to an important extent. Some psychoanalysts say that they have observed that thoughts which the agent is inclined to suppress are the very ones most likely to arise in the subject's mind.

On the occasion of another meeting, Mr. Alpha furnished a number of impressions which came to him while handling a cigar lighter, laid on the table by a member of the audience. Practically none of the impressions were acknowledged as correct. The experiment seemed to be a total failure. Mr. Alpha, however, kept insisting that what he saw had to be correct. A few days later I was visited by

Mr. W. v. E. He told me that an exchange of cigar lighters had taken place, of all things, a few days before the aforementioned meeting. The cigar lighter handled on that occasion really belonged to Mr. W. v. E. Practically all of the data furnished by the psychoscopist—several quite specifically—appeared to relate to Mr. v. E., who had not been personally present at the session.

When we study the criteria which form the basis for the awareness of correctness in Mr. Alpha and other psychoscopists, it becomes apparent to us that the clarity as well as the vividness of the images play an important role. The exclusiveness and persistency of the ideas forcing themselves upon the paragnost are likewise important.

If I am acquainted with two people who, let us say, are both named Klaassen, one of whom is a dentist and the other a composer, and supposing that while I am talking with somebody about a subject in the field of music the name Klaassen is brought up, then I shall have a number of ideas thrust upon me about the composer Klaassen, while ideas connected with Klaassen the dentist will remain in the background. Contrariwise, in a conversation about dentistry, if the name Klaassen comes up, the ideas associated with Klaassen the composer will stay in the background, and the totality of ideas about Klaassen the dentist will come to me.

Th. Ziehen has described the influence which the contents of the consciousness seem to exercise on recollections with the term "working of the psychic constellation." The working of the psychic constellation also comes up when, for instance, a psychiatrist instructs a patient to "focus" his attention on a certain event in his life. If the patient accepts this instruction, it will then create, as Ach says, a "determining tendency," which tendency in turn creates a certain psychic constellation.

If we now return to the psychoscopists, it is with the intention of pointing out that they can concentrate their minds not only on certain people or inductors, but also on certain events which occurred in the past (just to limit ourselves to one thing at a time) of these people. The following example will serve as an illustration.

It concerns a Mrs. M. H. at T. She suffered for a number of years from asthma, an ailment for which, according to her, she obtained insufficient relief from doctors. Accordingly, she turned to

Figure 1. The paragnost Gerard Croiset gives his impressions about a lost child over the telephone. The conversation is being taped automatically.

Figure 2. A police sergeant consults Croiset in the author's presence.

the "magnetizer"[12] Alpha, who was well-known not only as a "healer" but also as a paragnost. On her first visit, Mr. Alpha readily informed her that he had the impression that her asthmatic symptoms had a psychic origin and were connected with an experience in her youth. Whereupon, he says, he focussed his attention on her school years, and commented that he thought she must have had, in her final year of school, a shocking experience with another girl and a small knife. "I see blood," the paragnost said. "This must have caused you great agony."

Mrs. H. replied to this as follows:

> The day before the last day of school—I was then 13 years old—our class was allowed an hour of free drawing. One of my classmates and I stood by a coal-bin. I sharpened my pencil with a pocket knife belonging to the teacher. All of a sudden the knife flew out of my hand, with the result that the girl standing next to me received a cut on her arm, about 10-13 centimeters long and 1 centimeter deep. The fear and shock which I experienced were almost indescribable. But the punishment by the teacher which followed was worse than everything else put together. The teacher decided that I would not leave school, like the rest of the children, but demanded that I start all over again in the second grade on the following morning.
>
> School always having been something which frightened me very much, this seemed to make everything insurmountable. Of course, the teacher didn't mean it. The following day he changed his attitude towards me and everything came out all right. . . .

An analogous case was reported in my *Inleiding tot de parapsychologie*, page 181.

Not only an accidental conversation or an accepted instruction can lead to a certain psychic constellation. Studies in special psychology[13] have also disclosed determining tendencies connected with congenital as well as acquired psychic structure. On page 95 and following of my *Beschouwingen over het gebruik van paragnosten* ("Views on the Uses of Paragnosts") I reported the case of Mrs. S. She was a psychoscopist who often gave striking details about the sex lives of people entirely unknown to her, details which escaped other psychoscopists who were given the same inductors.[14] If we ask ourselves why only this psychoscopist could deliver this kind of data the answer can only be this: because her interest lay especially in the area of the sex lives of her consultants (whether personally present at the sitting or not). She had a need to "see" just those details, and now this need had been connected to her inborn and also to her acquired "character."

Mrs. S. was by nature a very temperamental and sensual woman. At a young age she married a man who in the sexual sense could not satisfy her. This marriage was dissolved through divorce. Afterwards, she had a series of unsatisfying relationships with men, predominantly married. She met them in a circle of artists. On top of that, as a child she had already witnessed conflicts, almost entirely of a sexual character, between her parents. One and the other led to the development of a psychic constellation, and she became known as a subject whose interest was directed, if not exclusively, then at least preponderantly towards sexuality.

I have observed similarly specialized interests, also of combined inborn and acquired character, in various of my subjects. Here I think for instance of Mr. Beta. In my experiments with this paragnost, it struck me that he was repeatedly able to give the exact birthdays of people, whether or not they were personally present at a sitting. This observation led me to suppose that a determining tendency of his, possibly from some experience undergone in his youth, gave rise to such a psychic constellation, which created favorable conditions for birthdates to come up in his mind.

A close investigation disclosed that my supposition was correct. As one of the oldest in a family of seventeen children, he had many times been in a situation of anxious expectation when the parental home was being made ready for the arrival of another little brother or sister, and the more so, because he had been told all kinds of alarming tales about birth. At such times he was boarded out with one of his grandmothers, and allowed to return home after the new little brother or sister lay in the cradle and his mother could resume her daily tasks. This return, which depended on a birthdate, and to which he had looked forward with longing, meant for him a freeing of terrifying thoughts which he endured in relation to his mother, to whom he was very affectionately attached.

Two other subjects, who could achieve exceptional results in tracking down lost or drowned children or adults, were found to have escaped from death by drowning in their youth by the skin of their teeth.

A large number of others might readily be added to these examples.

It will therefore be apparent that there are many reasons to suppose that the working of the psychic constellation is also revealed in telepathy. And this furnishes yet another argument in support of the thesis proposed by Heymans and others, according to whom telepathic phenomena can be considered as a kind of incoming thought.

Research into memory has shown that one of the factors on which the ability to reproduce events depends is the feeling which the perceptions and ideas may evoke. We all know from experience that the incidents which make a deep impression on us are indelibly inscribed, and as a rule (assuming that they have not been suppressed) are easily recalled.

Therefore, when in telepathy we deal with "inneren" we would assume that the impressions of the psychoscopists in a predominant number of cases are related to events they find exciting in the lives of their consultants, whether the latter are present or not. We give an example. On a certain day, one of my subjects accidentally met a Mr. X., whom he did not know. He got an image of a man, recognizably Mr. X., in a room, throwing a chair at a woman in an outburst of rage. The paragnost told Mr. X. what he saw and advised him to show a little more self-control in the future. Mr. X. had to confess that the image forcing itself spontaneously on the psychoscopist was an instance out of a scene which had erupted in his living room a couple of days earlier.

An investigation undertaken by me disclosed that among the total of emotion-evoking memories possessed by a consultant, certain ones are privileged to force themselves on the paragnost's "inneren." Although I have reported quite extensively about this in my *Beschouwingen over het gebruik van paragnosten*, I would like to cite an eloquent example. It concerns Mr. Delta. When he met Dr. H., an Austrian, for the first time at the Parapsychological Institute, the image of a wild stretch of broken or eroded rocks forced itself on the paragnost. Because the forcing up of this image was associated with some other impressions, the paragnost was led to ask Dr. H. if he had recently been in a wild stretch of rubble. "You were accompanied by a lady," he added, "and very depressed. This was enforced by gloomy weather."

Dr. H. could only answer the question in the affirmative. He told the others present that about three weeks earlier and while in a depressed mood, he had visited the Lechfeld, known as a wild stretch of broken, eroded rocks in Austria. The weather was gloomy and he was accompanied by a lady.

Now when we ask the question, 'Why, out of the multitude of Dr. H.'s memories, were just these thrust up to the paragnost?' the reason will become apparent when we learn something of the past of the subject. Mr. Delta was a political prisoner in Germany during the war years. In a mountainous area he had to push wheelbarrows filled with rubble uphill. A road was being constructed. On several occasions, he was mistreated by the overseers. Rubble stone consequently has a special meaning in his life.

This is another clear example of the psychic constellation, to which we have already devoted some time.

It was also pointed out earlier in Chapter I that the state of lowered consciousness level should be regarded as a state in which inhibitions are diminished. In such a state long-forgotten memories force themselves on us.

Now it appears that the condition of passivity (lowered consciousness level), as might be expected, can be considered to be at the same time a favorable circumstance for "inneren." Those who have observed psychoscopists have seen them reach a partially lowered consciousness level[15] during the sittings. This lowering is often so subtle that the layman does not notice it, but this does not mean that it cannot be objectively demonstrated.[16] In some subjects, this lowering goes far enough to justify use of the term "trance"[17] and to speak of somnambulists.[18]

Some subjects attempt to achieve a lowered level of consciousness by means of a crystal ball or a piece of glass. With this, we return to the subject of the "magic mirror," to which we called attention in Chapter I.

The use of the magic mirror to achieve a state of diminishing inhibitions and to stimulate the manifestation of paragnostic powers is mentioned repeatedly, not only in the ethnological literature but also by classical authors* and those of the Middle Ages.

---

* According to what we read in Genesis 44:5, Joseph made use of the magic mirror (a silver cup filled with water) to achieve a state of reduced inhibitions.

It is common knowledge among those who have experimented with them that even today paragnosts use the magic mirror to reach a lowered level of consciousness and thus bring about heightened telepathic receptivity.

Over the years I have often encountered professional "clairvoyants" who have sought to achieve a slackening of the cohesion of memory-images with the aid of a crystal ball, and like other experimenters I have often tried to promote the success of my experiments by letting my subjects (psychoscopists and others) stare at a crystal ball.†

Related to crystal gazing is so-called shell-hearing. In *shell-hearing*, one listens to the entotic murmur, which we all know from experience becomes stronger when one holds a sea shell against the ear. Doing this, one sometimes "hears" words being spoken. These words may have not only a psychoanalytical meaning, but sometimes also justify our use of the term *clairaudience* and so testify to the paragnostic powers of the hearer.

Like crystal gazing, shell-hearing has apparently been observed by ethnologists among primitive peoples just as it has been observed by parapsychologists in their subjects. J. Hyslop, for instance, tells of a paragnost who heard in a shell (which she held against her ear) words spoken by one of her acquaintances, who had said goodbye to her only about a quarter of an hour earlier, to a friend whom he met on the street. This paragnost had made telepathic tests with this acquaintance.

If, when discussing crystal gazing, we have reason to use the term (pseudo-) *hallucination,* then in shell-hearing it appears to me that use of the term *illusion* would be appropriate.

In crystal gazing the term *illusion* should be used if one has to take into consideration the possibility that impurities in the glass (air bubbles, etc.), or pleats in the black cloth on which the ball is placed, might contribute to the "seeing."

The same goes for those who make use of coffee grounds, the white of an egg, and similar much-derided methods. It is quite understandable that they make themselves the laughingstock of many, although on the other hand one should also realize that to a certain extent they perform the same function as the inkblots which the ingenious H. Rorschach introduced for psychodiagnostic purposes.

---

† Jeane Dixon.

That paragnosts attain a state of partially lowered consciousness level during experiments is demonstrated by their apparent inclination to think in images.

Herbert Silberer found that, with a lowering of the consciousness level, thinking in images occurs. Thoughts, which one mulls over, give way suddenly to visual images, in which ideas are depicted. Various psychologists have studied these slumber-images. Jaspers is one of them. He pointed out that often they cannot be distinguished from dream-images, and also fade from one into the other.

From the standpoint of genetic psychology, the image is the original language of our soul. When we become tired, or fall asleep, our spirit reverts to the original image-creating thinking, which is more primitive than thinking in words. Thus, we should regard our dreams as regression-phenomena, an opinion we find to be held by C. G. Jung and others.

Now the lowering of the consciousness level to which paragnosts are subject during experiments is consistent with the inclination to think in images. Those familiar with psychoscopists have often heard them express themselves in symbolic or picturesque ways. That the inclination to think in images often gives rise to mistakes speaks for itself.[19] With the development of thinking in words, we have become less and less accustomed to thinking in images. The paragnost is no more able to interpret his images correctly than we are always able to translate our dream-images. Thus, for example, one day a paragnost "saw" with an unfamiliar lady a case of Smyrna raisins. This hallucinatory experience led him to ask her if she liked to eat raisins. When she replied in the negative, the psychoscopist remarked that nevertheless, Smyrna raisins must have played a role in her life. The consultant then replied that she was born in Smyrna.

As we know that in former years this psychoscopist worked in a grocery store and continued to be interested in everything connected with this business, we can clearly see the *Verbildlichung* (image-forming) of the name of her birthplace. If, instead, he had been a postage stamp dealer, he would quite possibly have seen, in this instance, the image of a postage stamp with the word Smyrna on it.

The Psychology of the Paragnost

Although paragnostic phenomena are based on powers of general human nature, it seems nevertheless that paragnostic talent does not appear equally strongly in all people. At one extreme are those who are called telepaths and clairvoyants (paragnosts), and at the other those who say that during their entire lives they have perceived little or nothing of their paragnostic powers. In between, in slight gradations, are those who have had spontaneous paragnostic experiences once or several times during their lives, so they say.

It stands to reason that it is of great importance to undertake research into the personality structure of persons in whom paragnostic powers are revealed to a more than average degree. Several researchers have pleaded for the desirability of such research. I personally did so in 1926. Over the years, I have been able to collect an important amount of data in regard to temperament, character, and other details about psychoscopists (paragnosts). Since 1953, extensive experiments of both a psychodiagnostic and depth psychological nature have been carried on with psychoscopists and others at the Parapsychological Institute of the State University of Utrecht.[20]

As might have been expected on the basis of previous experiments, it has turned out that many are found among such persons who show a lack of interconnection between the various contents of consciousness. Heymans[21] rightly pointed out that these findings also support the thesis that in telepathy we are dealing with "inneren" because the slackening of the cohesion between ideas promotes the occurrence of thoughts without regard for whether they come from our own or from another's consciousness.

With the disintegration typical to a greater or lesser degree of so many paragnosts is associated a weakening of individuation. Already in C. G. Carus, who greatly influenced Ludwig Klages, we encounter the view that as individuation becomes weaker, the susceptibility to telepathic influence becomes greater. With this recognition, we enter the field of genetic psychology.

Genetic-psychological Reflections

Without going into the matter deeply, we will point out that a series of convergent arguments can be advanced in favor of the thesis that, phylogenetically speaking, extra-sensory perception preceded sensory perception. Most probably we should regard telepathy as a contact between people which can be called archaic. This archaic

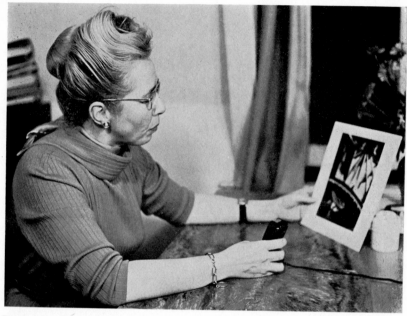

Figure 3. Psychodiagnostic examination of a subject by means of thematic apperception test (TAT).

contact, in the course of what is customarily called evolution (and which is revealed in Man as an increasing individuation and increasing intellectualism, among other things), is apparently supplanted by a contact on another level, which is consistent with the evolution of the sensory organs.[22]

In primitive Man and children this archaic contact is on the whole easier than in the adolescent or adult. Here we touch on a problem with which Ludwig Klages has dealt in such a fascinating manner in his important book *Der Geist als Widersacher der Seele* ("The Intellect as The Adversary of the Soul") and to which Bergson has also devoted attention. Further details are given in my *Inleiding tot de Parapsychologie*, and also in the chapter on paragnosis and empathy in my *Beschouwingen over het gebruik van paragnosten.*

Figure 4. Psychodiagnostic examination. The experimenter with a subject.

Chapter III

PROSCOPY

(future memory)

Positive Memory Disorders

THE OPPOSITE of negative memory disorders, which we discussed in Chapter I, are positive memory disorders, or *fausse reconnaissance* ("false recollection"). In fausse reconnaissance, unlike negative memory disorders, the new (unknown to us) seems to be already known. It provides us with what the French call *la sensation du déjà vu* ("impression of the previously seen").

A typical case of positive memory disorder was reported by A. Pick in *Archiv für Psychiatrie* (1876). It concerned an educated man who had much insight into his illness and who was able to give a good description of his ailment, which attacked him when he was about 32 years old. It seemed that whenever he went to a party, visited one place or another, or met someone, all of these events with their attendant details seemed so familiar that he thought he had surely experienced them before, with precisely the same persons and objects around him, with the same sky, the same weather. If he performed a new duty, it seemed to him as if it had happened before—that he had done it before under the same circumstances.

Cases of chronic sensation du déjà vu, based on obvious positive memory disorder, are rare. But this phenomenon often appears acutely. Several people have told us that they know this sensation from their own personal experience. For instance, the Italian medical man Majocchi, in his book *Surgeon*, describes the lying-in of a dying woman suffering convulsions caused by toxemia:

> I stood paralyzed by the sight of so much distress. Suddenly it seemed to me as if I had previously experienced such a moment. A heart-rending scene I had already seen before—but when and where? Then, suddenly, I remembered a powerful, majestic painting depicting the death of

[44]

Rachel, put on canvas by the magic brush of Cignaroli, that one can admire in the Royal Academy at Venice. It was the same scene, they were the same facial expressions, as those of the woman concerned.

I personally had a similar experience years ago. Self-analysis disclosed that a cut out print which I had received as a present in childhood was the cause of this sensation du déjà vu.

As we have seen, the phenomena of cryptomnesia and fausse reconnaissance are directly opposed to each other, yet according to Heymans they are closely associated.

> Both phenomena occur either simultaneously or alternately in the same individuals and also display the same correlations with qualities of temperament and circumstances; and it is also known that both occur with exceptional frequency during the puberal period and among epileptics.

Because in cases of depersonalization[1] a sense of familiarity is absent under circumstances where it should normally appear, and in fausse reconnaissance this sense of familiarity is forced upon one without there being a reason for it, many persons are quite understandably surprised when first told that, according to Heymans, both of these phenomena are closely linked to each other. It will be fully understood, however, if we examine his explanation carefully and accept Heymans' idea that fausse reconnaissance has as its basis *a more pronounced weakening of the associative activity of the contents of the perception.*

This supposition, according to Heymans, derives support from the fact that "fausse reconnaissance appears much more frequently than depersonalization and seems to be connected with qualities of temperament which favor the appearance of both phenomena." Heymans continues with the following:

> If now this supposition is correct, then what is experienced in a case of fausse reconnaissance must be distinguished in a characteristic way from what is seen in a case of depersonalization. In depersonalization, the stream of vague memories arising from a feeling of familiarity with the surroundings remains entirely absent. In fausse reconnaissance, however, these memories still make themselves count, but they are very weak, in undefined outline, with many gaps, or even given in only fragmentary form. From this it can be understood not only that depersonalization suggests a dream, but also that fausse reconnaissance gives the impression of recalling events into the awareness from a distant past.

For having seen and heard once again places, people, or melodies which we knew earlier, haven't we realized that the memories playing a part in it share the shadowy, incomplete quality shown in fausse reconnaissance?

According to this conception, in fausse reconnaissance we are also dealing not with too much, but just as in depersonalization with too little in the completion of the data by what is remembered. . . .

The illusion of too much originates in the fact that the contents of the consciousness of the moment are interpreted (without realizing it, of course) on the analogy of previous perception.

"Sensation du deja vu" and Proscopy

Although a number of cases of sensation du déjà vu can be explained without any reservation with the help of the hypothesis of positive memory disorder, it would of course not be permissible to generalize by claiming that all cases of this sort can be so explained. For the results of parapsychological research give us reason to allow that there are cases of sensation du déjà vu which are based on predictive dreams, forgotten or not, and related phenomena. To illustrate this, I will cite the following case of spontaneous paragnosis, reported to me by the Rev. Houtzagers (who had such an important part in the well-known ecclesiastical battle which was carried on in 1886 by A. Kuyper and colleagues). Rev. Houtzagers wrote the following:

It was in 1917. My nervous system was overwrought. I suffered from bad dizzy spells and because of them I had applied for my pension. Now it happened that on a Saturday afternoon I received an invitation from the commandant of the camp at Millingen to call on him on the following Wednesday afternoon at three o'clock to discuss the schedule of confirmation-classes. I had to give confirmation-classes each week to 400 soldiers in that camp. I did not know in which of the temporary buildings the commandant was quartered. Also, I had never met him. The only thing I knew was that he was rumored to be a rough, difficult man.

Sunday evening, after performing three services during the day, I lay half dreaming, resting on the couch. And then, little by little, the camp and the different camp roads came before my eyes. I walked through the camp, arrived at the quarters of the commandant, a building constructed of rough boards, with a kind of veranda. I looked for the entrance and found it underneath the veranda roof—swinging doors to a kind of indoor garden, in which stood two iron bedsteads. The door was obviously the main entrance, because there was a door-bell. I rang. A servant girl came, neatly dressed in black, with a lace apron and miniature cap on her head; she asked me to follow her. We walked on through, between the two bedsteads, and she took me into a well-kept living room, where the commandant was with his wife. Extremely polite and friendly, he advanced to meet me. We discussed the occasion for my visit. His lady offered me tea. She rang for the servant-girl. She came—it was the same one who had opened the door for me—and offered me a cup of tea on a small tray. At that very moment, as I tried to reach my hand out for the cup, I got quite a dizzy spell on my couch. With that, I seemed to sink away into a fathomless depth. On awaking again afterwards, I took this to have been a strange dream.

But now the disturbing part. Wednesday afternoon I went to Millingen. I did not think at all about Sunday, and now you must bear in mind that I never had seen the building, nor the persons of the commandant, his wife, or the servant-girl. When I arrived in that part of the camp, it affected me because I found myself exactly at the place I had seen Sunday on my couch. My emotions grew when I reached the house and saw the door under the veranda, and when on my ringing, it was opened by the same servant-girl. Once again she asked me to follow her, also between the two iron bedsteads. She led me to the commandant and his wife—exactly the same people, the same environment, the identical reception. And then I was seized by a great fear, when the lady also offered me tea, that I might become dizzy the way I did in my own room. When the maid brought me the tea, I controlled myself with all my might—and luckily the dizziness stayed away and my visit could go on without interruption.

I must tell you that, afterwards, I was deeply shaken. I could not understand how such a thing could be possible, three days before. I sought advice from a doctor, and he said: "We stand here before riddles..." Never again have I experienced such a thing and I'd say: "Luckily not!" In previous years, though, I sometimes had the feeling that I would get a letter from somebody, but never anything like that event in Millingen. . . .

Experience teaches us that during sleep we can undergo a paragnostic experience (dream) without necessarily remembering it on awaking (amnesia).[2] This means that we must keep in mind the possibility that under certain conditions a forgotten paragnostic dream can also be a cause for a sensation du déjà vu. Recognition of this fact not only justifies the principle which Freud wrote about concerning déjà vu,[3] but also adds something to it.

Predictive Dreams

The case reported by the Rev. Houtzagers was one of the countless examples of the so-called proscopic dream with complete (or at least reasonably close) congruity, which we have found reported in literature through the ages, and of which we have fully authenticated examples in modern parapsychological research.

To illustrate, I'll follow this up with a second example of a proscopic dream with complete (or at least reasonably close) congruity. It is taken from a booklet, *Some Cases of Predictions*, London, 1937, by Edith Lyttelton, published under the auspices of the British Society for Psychical Research. It concerned a Mrs. Pritchard, who married the Rev. Mr. G. Pritchard in 1920. This was a happy marriage. In 1922 she had an extraordinarily vivid dream which she related to several people. She dreamt that her husband died while preaching. She had to work her way through a great crowd of people. Behind velvet curtains, she found her husband lying dead.

On November 9, 1924 Rev. Mr. Pritchard commemorated the Armistice at the Pier Pavilion in the presence of 2500 people. Mrs. Pritchard sat with her stepdaughter in the rear of the hall, to the right. Never before had she heard her husband speak so eloquently. While she was looking up the closing hymn, somebody told her: "Your husband has fainted." She stood up and saw him being carried away from the makeshift pulpit. With her stepdaughter she struggled through the crowd. Behind hanging green velvet curtains lay the pastor. He had died.

Dunne-effects

It has been pointed out by Freud and his school that from the viewpoint of psychoanalysis, many dreams are linked with one or another impression from recent days, in many cases from the day preceding them. Freud called the impressions which act as dream inductors *Traumerreger*, a word which can be translated as "dream provokers." Now parapsychological research has disclosed that not only certain events from the near past, but also certain events from the near future can act as dream inductors.

When such events out of the nearby future provoke dreams, so-called proscopic dreams with fragmentary congruity develop. The dreams which develop from such unaccountable events out of the near future are analogous to dreams of the known, already experienced by us, and induced by one or another event out of the recent past (everyone knows such dreams from his own experience). J. W. Dunne was the first to study this type of dream systematically, and so the term *Dunne-effect* has been assigned to it. Like so many other people, I have observed the Dunne-effect in myself on more than one occasion.

I dreamed one night, for instance, that I was looking into the window of a bookstore. This shop window held a countless number of books by Karl May. They were laid out in rows. On awaking, I remembered this dream very keenly. A few hours later in my mail I received a prospectus from a publisher announcing the reprinting of a Dutch version of books by Karl May. One of the pages of this prospectus bore a lengthy series of books by this author, whom I so greatly enjoyed in my youth.

If I had had my dream after I received the prospectus, it could be readily assumed that it might have been the inductor for the dream. And similarly, in the light of the results of parapsychological research into proscopy, we feel justified in considering the prospectus as a dream provoker.

In the course of years, many people have reported about Dunne-effects. The material I have in my possession leads me to accept the Dunne-effect, like the telepathic dream, as a rather commonly experienced phenomenon.

Although no doubt the many occasional cases collected have contributed towards our knowledge of Dunne-effects, still it must be acknowledged that there is a possibility that among them there may be cases of accidental configurations not properly to be considered Dunne-effects. For that reason, the kind of systematic research performed by Messrs. Kooy and Kruisinga in the Netherlands and by Mr. C. F. Dalton in Ireland, whereby a statistical analysis of the material becomes possible, is to be preferred to noting down occasional Dunne-effects.

Dr. J. M. J. Kooy, now professor at the Royal Military Academy at Breda, discovered in 1932 that several times he had dreamed

about future events. This realization made a deep impression on
him. He studied the works of J. W. Dunne and got in touch with
me. The result was that he decided to investigate his dream life
precisely and to have this research controlled by me. For several
years, he painstakingly wrote down his dreams in duplicate.[4] In
addition, every day he carefully reviewed notes made on previous
nights and supplemented them with comments. By doing this, he
came to the conclusion that not only his recent past, but also his
nearby future were reflected in his dreams.

It has been stated that from the psychoanalytical viewpoint, the
chance that an event from the near past will become a dream provoker becomes greater to the degree that this event has a "hold" on
the person concerned. Our attitude towards incidents witnessed
during the day determines to a large extent whether or not they can
become dream provokers. Our attitude, in turn, depends on both
inborn and acquired traits.

In *Tijdschrift voor Parapsychologie*, VI, page 147, Doctor Kooy
reported that he lost his father through death in September 1932,
and that he was strongly attached to him and had great regard for
him. This death, after an unexpected illness lasting a couple of
months, made a very deep impression on him, and thus it is understandable that in the first year or so after his father passed away,
obituaries, funerals, announcements of severe illnesses, etc., very easily
gave rise to dreams. Now this is not only applicable to obituaries
and such things out of the recent past, but also to those from the
nearby future. In studying the material Doctor Kooy gave me, it
appeared to me that a significant part of his Dunne-effects concerned
future, incalculable cases of death and associated events. The following example will serve as an illustration. It was derived by me
from Doctor Kooy's controlled notes.

> *Dream Note, December 30-31, 1934.* I dreamed I traveled from
> the station at Apeldoorn to Huis ter Heide. I arrived there on a high
> railroad-embankment. The trees were lightly covered with snow. I con-
> cluded from the dream that Mr. C. P. v. R., who lived in Huis ter
> Heide, would die, because I had learned from past experience that
> snow in my dreams frequently symbolized death.* I rejected this con-
> clusion, however, because it seemed so entirely unrealistic to me.

---

* Not only black but white also is considered a mourning color. It symbolizes

On December 31 at 6:45 P. M. Mr. C. P. v. R. was struck by a train on the track at Huis ter Heide and killed instantly.** That I dreamt of the station in Apeldoorn is understandable when it is known that I myself was nearly caught once by a locomotive at that station. Mr. C. P. v. R. lived at Huis ter Heide. He was the only person I knew there.

It should be emphasized, however, that Doctor Kooy's Dunne-effects were not confined to cases of deaths, funerals, etc. As the next example shows, other incidents also brought them on. These were likewise "incidental" events which had an associative relationship with events in the life of the reporter.

Dream Note, August 30, 1933. A mixed-up dream story. I see a number of cars parked in a public square. I jump into a Ford, drive it back and forth a little with the brakes on and ruin them. After this, I damage the car some more, I don't remember exactly how. A bit later, I am running very fast, afraid the owner might come. There was also a friend involved in the dream. He looked at the damage I had caused.

This part of the dream note seemed to allude to events which actually happened during the course of the day following the night on which I had this dream. I drove to Epe, parked the car in the market-square behind a tree, and then went into the village. On the return trip the oil pressure seemed to have dropped off, and the pressure gauge didn't register any more. A check-up by an auto mechanic on the following day revealed, to my surprise, that three-fourths of the oil had disappeared from the crank-case of the car. Furthermore, greasy fingerprints were found on the body of the car, proving that some vandal had let the oil run partially out of it while it was unattended. However, the car in question was not a Ford but a Hupmobile.

As has been said earlier, Dunne-effects are predominantly concerned with the near future. Doctor Kooy published in *Tijdschrift voor Parapsychologie,* VII, page 276, a graph of 193 Dunne-effects, experienced in the course of two and one-half years, which showed that the overwhelming majority of those effects were borne out within

---

the enlightening which is thought to be conferred upon the departed. The hereafter is imagined to be a land of light.

** *Author's note.* I personally had a telepathic experience in regard to the accident. At the moment the accident occurred, a feeling of unimaginable sadness came over me. I knew something dreadful had happened, but not who was involved.

24 hours.* Also interesting are the graphs printed on page 80 in the 17th year edition of this journal. They demonstrate that, in order for Dunne-effects to be considered as incidental occurrences, and thus as pseudo-proscopic dreams, the curves would have to show a different character from what is actually the case.

It need hardly be added that the borderline between Dunne-effects and proscopic dreams with total congruity cannot always be sharply drawn, since there also are known to be proscopic dreams in which the congruity is more or less complete. These, therefore, should be regarded as an intermediate form between the two groups of proscopic dreams.

Allegorical Proscopic Dreams

There is yet a third category of predictive dreams. This group is comprised of those cases in which future events are shown in an allegorical manner. It is unnecessary to add that dreams falling into this category cannot always be distinguished from Dunne-effects. The following case will serve as an example of an allegorical proscopic dream. It concerns the unexpected passing away of Prof. K., as reported to me by his daughter, who is married to the German Senator Dr. H. H.[5] Mrs. H.-K. reported this dream to me a few days after the death of her father. Some weeks later, she confirmed some of the details in writing. In order to better understand the following, it is pointed out that psychoanalytical studies show that dying (to die, etc.) is often shown in a dream as "going on a journey," "leaving by train," etc. So it is understandable that in proscopic dreams (insofar as they may be concerned with cases of death), we repeatedly encounter this allegorical presentation. Mrs. H.-K. wrote the following:

> As I promised you, I'll now write down for you again what I pre-
> viously told you. It is about a dream I dreamed the night of the
> first or second day of Christmas in 1951. This dream is striking

---

* On the same pages are a second series of graphs. These concern J. C. M. Kruisinga, a notary, who also made notes of his dreams for a few years, and who likewise acknowledged that he repeatedly dreamed of certain future events. Notary Kruisinga, like the Irishman G. F. Dalton (see *T. V. P.* XXVI, pages 86 ff.) also could establish as a fact that Dunne-effects predominantly concerned the very near future.

because of the unexpected passing away of my father, Prof. Dr. H. K. on New Year's Eve in a car while on the way to the railroad station at Ermelo. He wanted to go to Brussels with my mother to spend New Year's Eve with the family of my youngest sister. I received a letter from this sister, in which she wrote about this plan on Thursday, December 27. I did not know anything about this on the night of the dream.

I myself have been living for about a year and a half in Berlin with my husband, the Senator (Minister), and our five children. On the way to church on the second day of Christmas, I recounted the dream to my three oldest children, aged 20, 18, and 17. There are thus three witnesses, so there is no possibility of my having made a mistake with this report, or of my having added or subtracted something from it later on. I give you the report without commentary, just as I told it to my children on the 26th of December.

Here is what I told them: "Imagine, how strange. I believe that for as long as I have been married, I have never dreamed of father or mother. And last night I dreamed about them so vividly. Listen to this"—and then I told the dream, positively as an excuse and with a feeling of shame for holding their attention with nothing more interesting than just a dream. I added, "Isn't it crazy?" Usually after awaking a dream is rather vague. But I really saw all this still very clearly. I mean that, for me, this dream always had a different quality from an "ordinary" one.[6]

Now then: I had to get into the railroad station, but the man at the barrier would not let me pass. He wanted to "see papers." Not my ticket, but papers. I could not understand this at all, because what kind of papers besides your ticket would you need to get into a station? Finally I said very impatiently—and while I said that I was sorry, because my husband gets irritated when I say such things and I'll do it only when I absolutely want to get my way—"See here, I am the wife of Senator H. and I won't negotiate with underlings. I shall go to the highest authorities." And thereupon I went to the manager of this colossal enterprise. The manager was extraordinarily friendly to me. It was really remarkable how friendly he was, and he said, "Oh, lady, we'll straighten that out immediately for you." And so I got into the station. It was, as I said, an enormous station with a number of platforms that I had to cross and then suddenly— imagine—there I stood face to face with father. Really—father, with his black hat, and his coat a bit shabby, and his brief case under his arm. "Father!" I called out, most pleasantly surprised. And father said (exactly the way Opa does, eh boys?)—very very friendly, but a little absent-mindedly, as if he was too busy with his own work— "So, child"—Opa always said in such a sweet voice, "So, child," didn't he? "So, child, nice to see you, but I cannot stay any longer now, I haven't any time left. I can't talk with you now, for I have to go." And as he said that, he stepped into his own separate train. This one stood absolutely apart on a separate railway track with the locomotive on the left end; and all the other trains and people, everything moved to the right.[7] And as he stepped into this train—just like Opa, so absorbed in the work awaiting him, so intent, that so to speak, he was not "with me" at all—he turned once more to me and said, "But go now to mother, because she is entirely alone, outside on the station square."

I went to the station square. Nobody else, only my mother was there. A large empty square and my mother walking there, away from the station. I saw her small back, lonely, the way someone who is alone looks. And as she walked, she pulled the handle of a sort of farm cart, like we used to have in Ermelo as children, and the four small children of my youngest sister in Brussels were in the cart, which she dragged behind her. Twice I called very loudly, "Mother!" but she did not hear it, at least she did not turn to look, and she disappeared with the cart around a corner in the direction in which everything and everybody except father's train was moving—to the right.

And now you might suppose that the coloration of the dream was sad, because it really was sad. First, I meet father for the first time after such a long, eventful period, a year and a half of profound experiences for me and him, and he has no time, and then I call twice "Mother!" and she does not hear me. But I was not sad. On the contrary, something radiant, something refreshing came forth from this dream, because suddenly I knew very clearly, differently from ever before (I can only say: in an existential experience) that, yes, all that now lies behind you. That's where you came from, that was your origin, that you carry also within you. But all that does not hurt any more, that "no time" and that "not hearing," because now I am on my way to Germany, on my way to my husband Herbert. There is my home now, there am I rooted.

When, on New Year's Eve, my husband brought me the telegram from Ermelo reporting our father's passing, my first thought was: That dream. That was a real meeting. Father and I really did say good-bye to each other that night. Or rather, I to him, at this last meeting, because he went, too purposeful to say good-bye or to linger in the moment. And besides—his instructions about mother. And when mother said, in church at the funeral, that no doubt he went without hesitation. And that if he had known that he was dying, his last words would have been, "What will happen to Ann?" Then I knew for sure that this was so, that it had happened that way and indeed that his only last thought was—even if it did not hold him back from going away—that thought about mother. Why mother did not hear my call I still cannot understand. Nor the meaning of the farm cart with the grandchildren from Brussels—or is it enough to think there is a connection with that journey they had wanted to make to Brussels on New Year's Eve, and finally did not make? Has the whole matter of "station and journey" something to do with that, or has it only a symbolic meaning?

Concerning the first part of the dream, the difficulties with the papers, so far I haven't made any reference to it. Throughout the entire day of January 2nd we were busy getting our papers in order. The three older children had to have passes which had to come from Bonn, and under normal circumstances this requires about six weeks. We had to have Dutch visas, and interzone passes to cross the Russian border. If my husband had not been "Senator" and I "Frau Senator," it would have been impossible. It was only so because of the very special friendliness of the highest authorities. The Dutch consul-general brought us our visas at half-past ten in the evening. To do it he drove by car for an hour and a half through Berlin, going to different departmental chiefs who had to stamp them. The head of the Berlin police sent motorized police on the morning of the third to pick up our passes at our home—they still had to be stamped once more—and the police delivered them to us at the station at a quarter to eight, our train being due to depart at eight-thirty. Only then, when we sat good and ready in the moving train, the first part of my dream hit me, to my great surprise. Thus, this also was not arbitrarily, not accidentally, but absolutely true. This journey was only possible because the highest authorities were so specially obliging. Last but not least remains, in my opinion, a very important part of my dream: finding my place. This deep, by its coloration, "new" knowing. I belong to Herbert. My home no longer is the Netherlands. I am invulnerable there, I carry that within me. There I came forth from. My home is now with my husband. There I am rooted. . . . The joy over this realization of life has lasted all these weeks. In an inexplicable sense, it is connected for me also with the previous happenings. It seems almost an instruction from father—this acceptance of one's own consequences, coming out of a decision of life. [I realize, is the greatest gift I got from both father and mother together in my life. It is the quintessence of both their lives. This became clearer in *his* going away and the way *she* accepted staying behind. In this way, I have accepted better than ever before the spiritual inheritance which I received from them—this joyful certainty of leaving behind what lies behind me, to be *home* with the man I chose, in a very different, very strange world.]

The entire dream, except for the first part, can of course be conceived as having a depth psychological meaning. One of my sisters whom I told it to tried to do this. There is only one answer to that: it is a mistake. It was not a subjective but an objective experience. It might be all that, but it is *also more* than that alone. Even the latter part, which of course had a strong depth psychological strain in my conclusion that "I belong with my husband," yet it also has besides a parapsychological quality; it could not be detached from the tie with father, it was associated with consequence to a new situation. I cannot describe this any clearer than that.

I hope that I have made clear to you what might be significant for you in this dream and the events connected with it. Because it had such an objective meaning for me, I almost felt prompted not to keep it to myself, quite otherwise than with every other dream,[8] and I am thankful for being allowed to report this to you. . . .

Do we possess knowledge about our own future?

Schiller, in *Wallenstein's Tod,* Canto V, Stanza III, put the following words in Wallenstein's mouth:

> *Es machte mir stets eigene Gedanken,*
> *Was man vom Tod des vierten Heinrichs liest:*
> *Der König fühlte das Gespenst des Messers*
> *Lang vorher in der Brust, eh' sich der Mörder*
> *Ravaillac damit waffnete, ihn floh*
> *Die Ruh, es jagt ihn auf in seinem Louvre,*
> *Ins Freie trieb es ihn, wie Leichenfeier*
> *Klang ihm der Gattin Krönungsfest, er hörte*
> *Im ahnungsvollen Ohr der Füsse Tritt,*
> *Die durch die Gassen von Paris ihn suchten.**

* "That which we read of the fourth Henry's death
　Did ever vex and haunt me like a tale
　Of my own future destiny. The king
　Felt in his breast the phantom of the knife
　Long ere Ravaillac armed himself therewith.
　His quiet mind forsook him; the phantasma
　Started him in his Louvre, chased him forth
　Into the open air; like funeral knells
　Sounded that coronation festival;
　And still with boding sense he heard the tread
　Of those feet that even then were seeking him
　Throughout the streets of Paris."
　　　　　　—translated by Samuel Taylor Coleridge

We shall not concern ourselves here with the question whether this case of foreknowledge is an historical fact, but limit ourselves to observing that Schiller apparently was already acquainted with the fact that there are reasons for accepting the idea that man, in his "deepest being," knows his own future. Leibniz pointed out that this foreknowledge usually reveals itself so weakly that we perceive little or nothing of it.[9]

C. G. Carus, that last and greatest of the psychologists of the Romantic period, in lectures delivered during the winter of 1829-1830, called attention to the fact that some people have unmistakable premonitions about their approaching deaths and can announce them. This friend and personal physician to Goethe is certainly not the only medical man to have described this remarkable fact. Various parapsychologically-oriented doctors have reported on invalids who, in line with their own but contrary to their physicians' expectations, died of one or another illness for which they had sought the help of these physicians. Osty, the French physician and parapsychologist, is one researcher who has repeatedly pointed out in his publications that there are patients who seem to possess an unmistakable foreknowledge as to the outcome of their illness. He reported a number of cases of patients who died of illness following their premonitions, completely against the expectations of their doctors, whom they had asked for help and who considered their condition far from alarming.

Although Osty rightly took into account the possibility that, in a number of cases, the rock-firm belief of the forecaster might have led to the realization of his self-predicted death,[10] Osty is nevertheless of the opinion, and I can completely agree with him, that we would be going too far to ascribe all of such instances of death to auto suggestion. Osty is the more of that opinion, because of these instances of self-predicted death, which are difficult to explain away; each case should not be judged on its own, but in relation to and against the background of other such cases. Those who are oriented in parapsychological literature are acquainted with many cases of this kind. One such was reported to me in 1954 by the late evangelist, H. Boschma.

My youngest brother also was apparently paragnostically talented.[11] I happened to be home on vacation when he also arrived on leave as a non-commissioned officer in the Dutch colonial army. Because our parents were cramped for room, we had to sleep together in an old-fashioned Frisian bedstead. There was a so-called bedshelf above the footboard of the bedstead. Besides serving an understandable purpose, it was used as a place to store all sorts of things, for which it is hard to find any other place in a small house, so as to have them ready at hand.

In the middle of the night, my brother suddenly started up, stood up straight on the bed, and thrashed around and about like a fencer, so that all the miscellaneous things on the bedshelf flew about the bed and the room, while he yelled: "Go on and shoot, chaps, go on, shoot!"

I quieted him down with difficulty. When he awoke, he didn't remember it at all.[12]

He left for Indonesia, came on leave again and remarked, when he said goodbye, that he had a hunch that this time he'd stay there. Six months later we received word that he had died as the result of wounds suffered in a fight against the Atjehians. We did not then know of the circumstances. A few months later we learned the following details.

The Netherlands government had seen another chance to embitter[13] the "pacified" population of Atjeh, so the inhabitants of various villages decided they'd sooner leave everything behind and move inland. This, however, was not allowed unless they obtained passes, and the military authorities had been instructed to prevent illegal moving.

At one side of the main route inland there was a small fort, almost completely surrounded by a swamp, a narrow path serving to connect the road with the fort. The garrison consisted of a couple of native corporals and about twenty soldiers under my brother's command. All of a sudden my brother spotted the approach of a band of Atjehians with their belongings under their arms. He ordered the garrison to cover him and went up the path to ask the leader of the group for his pass. Instead of reaching into his bosom, where he would carry that paper, this man seized his *klewang*, a large knife. My brother shot him down before he could bare it. Immediately, though, twenty or thirty men came rushing at him with klewangs. He withdrew on the path, shooting down one after another. But finally the fingers of his left hand were chopped off, and thus the gun fell from his hand. Then he pulled out his klewang with his right hand. And all the while he yelled to his men, "Go on, shoot, chaps, go on, shoot!" But they could not fire, because they would have hit him, too. Finally, he lost his klewang also. Then he jumped into the swamp, and immediately came the reports of the shots from the fort, which drove his attackers to their heels.

My brother was pulled out of the swamp, wounded in twenty-two places, and died two days afterwards.

An analogous case is cited in my *Beschouwingen over het gebruik van paragnosten*, page 130. It concerns the poet Dr. H. J. Marsman, who as appears from his poem *Maannacht* ("Moonnight"), published in 1934, (and also from reports by his wife) foresaw his own violent death (1940) ten years in advance.

Such foreknowledge, which can exhibit varying degrees of clarity,[14] is by no means limited to one's own death. Deaths of others can also be involved, as might be interpreted from examples given earlier. It seems, furthermore, from the material we have on hand that, besides death, foreknowledge can be concerned with countless other events, both important and unimportant. There is almost no event imaginable, which in principle it should not be possible to foresee.

Occasionally someone dreams the winning number of a lottery ticket. A well-documented instance of such a lottery dream is found in *Tijdschrift voor Parapsychologie*, 16th year, page 182. It concerns Mr. H. J. F. R. of Roermond, who dreamed in November 1947 that a large prize would fall on ticket number 3684 of the States lottery. He got in touch with Mrs. A. B.-R., an agent for the States lottery at Roermond, who with some difficulty succeeded in getting hold of the ticket which Mr. R. wanted. In March 1948 a prize of 25,000 guilders fell on the lottery ticket requested by Mr. R.

Precognitive Telepathy

If we return yet once again to the psychoscopists, it is in order to point out that their impressions are not limited absolutely to the present and past of their consultants, but also very often concern their future.

As illustrations, I shall give two examples concerning the paragnost Mr. Eta, with whom I have been acquainted for several years and who, on the basis of his performance and reliability enjoys the trust of many in this country.

The first case concerns Mr. X., an accountant, who consulted Mr. Eta on March 3, 1955. Following a change in the management of the business in which he was then employed, he was put on half-pay. He had looked in several places for a position suitable for him. On the advice of one of his business associates, who said he had consulted this psychoscopist a few times with success, in mid-February he requested a consultation with Mr. Eta.

The consultation took place on March 3. There follows a summary of a report drafted by Mr. X. on April 27 on the basis of notes taken by him on March 3.

Words of the psychoscopist	*Comment*
1. I see you work with books.	Mr. X. is an accountant, and as such works with office books.
2. You did not choose your occupation with pleasure. Your talent is such that you would have done better in the practice of law.	After his final secondary school examinations, Mr. X. by chance went to work in an accountant's office. He continued in that line. Later, he thought of changing careers, but had never done anything about it. It struck him quite often that he possessed a flair for legal problems.
3. You have a good intellect.	A psychodiagnostic examination showed that Mr. X. can be regarded as intelligent.
4. But you also have a good intuition. I could even say that, to a certain degree, you are a clairvoyant!	Mr. X. noted here: "This is correct. In my daily life I follow my intuition once in a while. I have never regretted it. Now and then it happens that I can spontaneously predict something to others. Those are, however, always short-term predictions. I cannot predict at will."
5. You are good at giving guidance.	Organizing is in Mr. X.'s blood. He has been unjustly accused of meddling.
6. You must not go overseas.	Mr. X. applied for a position in South America, but withdrew his application for certain reasons, and a dislike of being away from home for so long.
7. You should not go into business for yourself. But if you do, you must have a good partner. You have to get someone who can "ride roughshod," because you cannot collect certain outstanding accounts. For the rest, your work is excellent.	Just then, Mr. X. was having great difficulty in collecting some outstanding accounts. His debtors realized, however, that his work was excellent.
8. Just now, people in your home and you also are irritable.	Quite right.

9. You have two children, you could have had three.

Mr. X. is the father of two children. About two years ago his wife had a miscarriage. Mr. X. and his wife never speak about it.

10. Your wife is quickly affected by unpleasant things. Don't tell her too much. Conceal unpleasant experiences from her as much as possible.

Unpleasant news affects Mrs. X. very much. Right away, she'll "have a fright." However, Mr. X. still tells her too much.

11. Your wife is bothered a lot by headaches.

Correct.

12. I see only one of your two children. He is a lively, blond boy with a good intellect. He learns easily. He will study later. You'll get a lot of pleasure from him.

Mr. X.'s younger son is nine years old. He is blond and lively. He learns easily. The elder is 14. He is dark. Although he has a good intellect, he doesn't learn well.

13. Your hard times are finished and you are on the eve of an important improvement.

Through a combination of circumstances, Mr. X. had had some difficult years. On March 20, seventeen days after the consultation, he was appointed accountant in an extremely large business. This offered him good opportunities.

14. You'll get in touch with a big man. A little man is in his presence.

Three days after the consultation, Mr. X. met both of these persons (in connection with his application) See 15.

15. You'll have a discussion. It will take place in the evening, if I see right. It seems that you'll go home with a contract.

On March 17, exactly 14 days after the consultation, the predicted discussion took place in the afternoon, not in the evening hours. On March 17 in the morning, Mr. X. was called on the telephone. Three days later, the signing of the contract took place. The director was a corpulent man, quite big. The co-worker in the legal department was smaller. See 14.

16. I see you in the midst of a big festival. I see a lot of flags around you. I would not know if this has anything to do with your position or not, but you surely are the focal point.

By coincidence, Mr. X. was involved in a big festival with a lot of flowers and flags. He had to give a speech to some hundreds of people present for the occasion. This had nothing to do with his position. This prediction was realized on March 12.

17. There is a great improvement for you in the future. At the end of the month you are going to be in entirely different and better circumstances than at present.

On March 17, fourteen days after the consultation, this prediction came true.

18. I see you in a big office. You go in and out. You have a brown bag, not the black one you have with you now.

The office where Mr. X. got his position was very large. More than 100 people were working there. Originally, Mr. X. carried a black bag. Later on, he changed it for a brown one.[15]

19. You are going to have many discussions. Now and then books enter into them.

Correct. In connection with a new sphere of action.

20. You'll select your friends.

Mr. X.: "Absolutely correct! I am very busy with that."

21. Keep quiet! There are would-be friends with secretly hostile intentions. They want to know everything about your former life, so as to misuse it later.

Mr. X. noted here: "Totally correct. I have already observed this in my business. One tried with so-called good intentions to find out everything about my past."

22. . . ..

Here the paragnost amplified some data about the rest of Mr. X.'s life. We can omit these because they cannot be verified yet.

The second case concerns the family of Mrs. W. R. at D., who reported the following to me in 1955:

In the summer of 1929 we came into contact with Mr. Eta through one of our friends, Mr. G. H. On the occasion of the consultation which resulted from this meeting, Mr. Eta told me that although I thought that the care of children was a thing of the past for me, that this was not at all the case. "I continue to see you surrounded by children," Mr. Eta said. "They are all very friendly towards you, and they are all carrying things in their hands or on their backs." When I asked him how old these children were, he answered, "From about nine to quite grown up; yes, even adults are there, too."

I didn't understand anything about this prediction. A few years later, though, my husband and I were invited to assume the management of a youth hostel at Arnhem. While we were in this youth hostel, we had quite a lot to do with children and young people. The vision of Mr. Eta came true.

Not long after this consultation Mr. Eta visited us in our home on the Graaf Ottolaan at Oosterbeek. We took a stroll in the neighborhood and noticed that Mr. Eta became quite anxious. He asked how we could stand that environment, for he had visions of all kinds of murder and manslaughter. He also heard ghastly sounds. When we were back at the house, Mr. Eta continued seeing all kinds of images there. First he described a young man with a crooked back, who cursed appallingly. The description fitted a boyhood friend of my brother, who died years ago. Mr. Eta also told us that we became acquainted with this young man when he was seven years old. This also was correct.

I went upstairs with Mr. Eta to my husband's room. There he once again became very anxious and said: "Oh, look out there at the windows of the garage. I see soldiers in uniforms of a kind we don't know. They stand huddled over something, it looks like an ordnance-map. It is terrible here, it is worse here than on the other side of the grounds of the Johanna-hoeve." A little later Mr. Eta urged my husband, "Oh, Mr. R., do leave this place, and take everything you own to safety. It is awful here." We could not understand a thing. Mr. Eta said further to my husband (who had once built several houses near our home) that he should not build any more in the future. "I see you going into a kind of mosaic business with your son. But here, one just cannot stand it."

Now we moved away from there, not on the advice of Mr. Eta, but because, as already related, we were put in charge of the management of the youth-hostel. We lived then for some time in "a big house with a large balcony" as Mr. Eta had predicted. After living in that big house with that large balcony from 1930 to 1933, we moved to Zuilen. By coincidence my husband became associated with a firm that manufactured parquet flooring. Thus my husband and my son entered the flooring business, in which my son has continued up to the present. There is an efficient workshop in the garden of the house we now live in. Thousands of square yards of parquet flooring are manufactured in it. Mosaic floors are poured in the same place. Thus, Mr. Eta had had a very accurate image of the future.

In 1944 the fighting in the vicinity of Arnhem was horrifying. The houses my husband had built in Oosterbeek, including the one in the Graaf Ottolaan, were destroyed. They did not belong to us any more, because my husband had sold them. During the fighting those houses were held now by the British, now by the Germans. The Germans and English were literally cutting each others' throats. On the grounds of the Johanna-hoeve also, the fighting was dreadful.

I must add further that when Mr. Eta visited us, we also called at the home of one of my friends, Mrs. X. Her husband had left a year earlier for Surabaya, where he had an excellent position. The plan was for his wife with her little four-year-old daughter to join him after a while. Mr. Eta predicted that Mrs. X. would go to Indonesia and described the house that they were going to live in. This description later seemed to be correct. However, Mr. Eta did not seem able to foresee very far for Mrs. X. Although he also became very anxious in her company, he could not see the cause of it. Mrs. X., who led a life free of excitement until the war with Japan, died later in a Japanese camp. Did Mr. Eta receive an impression about that, when he became so anxious?[16]

Granted that, "in his deepest being," every human knows his own destiny, which is useful as a working hypothesis, then it may be supposed that the predictions of psychoscopists are based, if not exclusively then predominantly, on precognitive telepathy. In other words, it seems reasonable to suppose that psychoscopists obtain their knowledge about the future of their consultants by means of telepathy from their consultants' "future memories."[17]

Predictions about Communities

The vicissitudes of communities are reflected in the vicissitudes of the individuals comprising them. In connection with an inquiry which I undertook into the spontaneous occurrence of paragnostic phenomena, Mr. L. L. of The Hague, whom I knew personally and who spent much of his life in Indonesia, reported the following to me in 1948:

> When it began I cannot say, because at first I did not pay any attention to it. But the same dream returned every now and then, and that's the reason why it has been imprinted so strongly in my memory...
> Nor do I know exactly how often I had that dream. I should say at least fifteen times in the course of about ten years. It resembled a memory dream of my army days, yet with remarkable differences, which I explained by the well-known fact that so often, dreams don't seem to have a regular sequence or logical connection.
> Later on it became apparent that the dream had a predictive character.
> And now for its contents. Except for the remarkable differences I mentioned earlier, the dream would have been a true reproduction of what I had experienced a couple of times each day during my term of military service, before I became a corporal.
> I stand in formation. The commands go: "Attention. Right dress! Eyes front! Count off! Parade rest!" Rollcall is taken.
> "Attention! Forward, march!"
> That's all. But now the differences. 1. We are not ranked according to height, as in the army. 2. We are not in uniform and don't even wear the same clothes. On the contrary, we form a many-colored rabble. All of us in civilian clothes, not too neat, and no two of us dressed alike. 3. We don't stand still after the command: 'Attention!,' but move and talk with one another. 4. Although I was discharged from the army as a sergeant, and if I had to make a formation again, I should have to stand on either the right or left wing, in the dream

I stand in the middle and seem not to have a rank higher than the others.

When the dream came back again and again, and I could remember each of the details longer and better, I noticed myself that I never had gone through a formation in such a manner. It was not a memory-image. But I didn't consider by a long shot that there was a possibility that the dream could carry a prediction. I could not conceivably get into such circumstances, in view of the fact that I had a well-patronized business, some money in the bank, a couple of houses, and furthermore that my age exempted me from every military or public service.

And yet, all this turned out to be literally true.

On the first day of my internment by the Japanese in Indonesia, I went through this exactly as I had repeatedly dreamed it over the years. It was so "true to the dream," I could have imagined being back in the dream, if I were not so certain of the bitter reality of the situation.

And what is also characteristic, from that moment on the dream never once returned.[18]

Here we are faced with one of those innumerable proscopic dreams which, despite the fact that it bore a strictly personal character, yet reflected the fate of the community of which the dreamer was a part. The dream of Mr. L. contained an indirect prediction of war.

In my book *Oorlogsvoorspellingen* (1948) containing the results of an inquiry into the extent that the second world war was "foreseen," various examples are given of such indirect predictions of war. Also, as I showed elsewhere,[19] H. Marsman's poem *Maannacht* can serve as a well-authenticated example of an indirect prediction of war.

Now, if we grant that psychoscopists can obtain knowledge by paranormal means from their consultants' future memory (precognitive telepathy), we may also expect many other known cases in which it seems undeniable that psychoscopists are able to become aware in an indirect way about something of the future vicissitudes of the communities of which their consultants are a part. This expectation is borne out not only in the contents of my book cited above, but in the writings of other researchers as well. Thus, the French doctor and parapsychologist, Dr. E. Osty, for one, pointed out in his book *La connaissance supra-normale*, with several examples, that numerous persons consulting psychoscopists in the years before the outbreak of the first world war had gotten predictions from which the outbreak as well as the course of the war could be deduced.

It is not necessary to argue that the indirect predictions of the psychoscopists are restricted to wars, for natural catastrophes, strikes, fires, business incidents, traffic accidents, and other events involving greater or smaller groups of people can also be deduced from predictions of psychoscopists.

Thus, for instance, I have reported in my *Beschouwingen over het gebruik van paragnosten*, page 140, the noteworthy case of Mr. S., the manager of a large bakery in Utrecht. On March 26, 1953 he came by coincidence into contact with the psychoscopist Alpha, who predicted, more or less spontaneously, that he would receive very important orders for rusk (baby food) from Sweden within a few weeks. Alpha also visualized the design that would be on the wrapping material. Mr. S. thought it unlikely that this prediction would come true. The more so, because the volume of orders his factory was receiving from Sweden had gone down. He asked Mr. Alpha if he possibly meant cakes. The psychoscopist replied that he clearly saw rolls of rusk. On that same day, Mr. S. told me about this prediction, commenting that there was little chance it would be realized. A few weeks later, there was a widespread strike of bakers in Sweden. As a result, Mr. S. received large orders for rusk. Because the Swedish government evidently did not want to influence the course of the strike, orders for cake were suspended during that time.

It seems to me that this case might be considered to be an indirect prediction of a strike. Mr. S. would not have received these big orders had not the bakers' strike broken out in Sweden.

Inasmuch as it would be acceptable to consider that in this example, Mr. Alpha had obtained his information from Mr. S.'s psyche by paranormal means (precognitive telepathy), it would be entirely possible, of course, that Mr. S. had produced a proscopic dream about the Swedish orders for rusk which awaited him.

The following case will serve as an example of an indirect prediction of a natural catastrophe. It concerns Mrs. L. G., who dreamed during the night of January 25-26, 1953 that her sister and brother-in-law, who lived in Zierikzee, came to stay with her. When she recalled her dream upon awaking, she took note of the fact that they were very shabbily dressed. She kept thinking about the dream during the entire day, and contrary to her usual behavior, talked to others about the dream which seemed "unforgettable" in contrast to her other dreams.[20]

A few days later, on February 1, 1953, Mrs. G.'s sister and brother-in-law were driven from their home by a storm flood. They were hospitably sheltered by Mrs. G. for quite an extended period of time. In a conversation with me, my informant rightly pointed out that, in the shabby clothing which her sister and brother-in-law wore in the dream, there was an allegorical presentation of their loss of lock, stock, and barrel suffered in the flood disaster.

In further support of our suggestion that in a majority of instances, if not always, psychoscopists obtain their knowledge of the future of their consultants in a paranormal way from their "future memory," another experiment of the French researcher Osty, already mentioned, should be reviewed.

In November 1915 he asked one of his subjects, a Mme. Morel, to tell him something about the course of the first world war. She told him she could not do it. Then, starting from the hypothesis that in his "deepest being," every human knows his own future, Osty asked her to tell him what *he* would know in future about the course of the war. Thus, Mme. Morel received instructions to draw from Osty's "mémoire future." This she was able to do quite remarkably, as was proven by the fact that she then made some predictions, especially concerning Greece, which if they were correct, could be verified during the ensuing months. Among the predictions made by the paragnost on this occasion was one which, although it proved to be wrong, demonstrated convincingly that, if not in all then still in the majority of cases, psychoscopists get their knowledge of future nondeducible events from the "mémoire future" of the persons with whom they are in telepathic contact.

The prediction I have in mind concerned Constantine I, then King of Greece, who in those days was favorably disposed towards the Germans, in contrast with his ministers Venizelos and Panos. Mme. Morel "saw" an attempt to kill the king being perpetrated in his palace by a woman who was very close to him. The assassination never took place. Afterwards, however, it appeared that the rumor was current and, according to Osty, also reported in the newspapers, that Queen Sophia had perpetrated an attack on her husband. She despised him because of his inertia, and thought it would be for the good of the country if he disappeared from the political scene. The rumor of the attempt on the life of the King perpetrated by the Queen thus came to pass, and was believed by Osty in the days when it was current.

Are there cases of direct predictions about communities? Up to now, I have continually hesitated to say that psychoscopists *always* get their knowledge about the future from the psyches of their consultants. Thus, it may be inferred that I do not rule out the possibility of cases of proscopy in which it is out of the question for the paragnosts to derive their knowledge from their own or another's "future memory."

Therefore the question arises whether cases of this kind are known, which would require us to determine the existence of something like a superindividual "mémoire future."

In order to answer this question, we should check to see if there are any known predictions about our era made in previous ages. Such predictions must have been made so long ago that none of the contemporaries of the paragnosts are still alive, in order for it to be out of the question for them to have come by their knowledge from an individual "future memory."

In my *Oorlogsvoorspellingen,* I have indicated that, so far, literary research has provided us with too small an amount of useful data to provide a scientifically responsible answer to this question. At most, it can only be said that these data reinforce the idea that material of this kind needs to be expanded.

Time and Space

Here I cannot go into the question of an explanation for the occurrence of predictions. It must suffice to point out that the phenomena of clairvoyance in space and time, like those of telepathy, compel us to reexamine our naive "realistic" views about space and time. Kant has already indicated that they are untenable. Further, see my *De Voorschouw.*

Chapter IV

POSSESSION AND GHOST-SEEING

("inneren" of what the deceased could remember during their life on earth)

"Co-feeling"

Mrs. J. R. Severn, wife of the well-known English painter, reported that she woke up one morning with the feeling that she had just been slapped hard on the mouth. This impression was so vivid, she took her handkerchief and pressed it against her mouth, absolutely sure that her upper lip was injured. This not being the case, it slowly began to dawn on her that she had only dreamed all this. Reasoning further, she was more and more convinced that it was impossible for anything to have harmed her. She looked at her watch and saw it was seven o'clock. As her husband was not in the room, she concluded correctly that he must have gotten up very early to go sailing. She met him at the breakfast table at about eight thirty. She noticed that he furtively pressed his handkerchief against his lip in the same way she had done at seven o'clock that morning. When she asked him what the matter was, he told her that around seven o'clock that morning he had received a sharp blow on the upper lip from the tiller. A sudden squall had come up and unexpectedly whirled it at him. "It bled quite a bit and it wouldn't stop," Mr. Severn added.

Here we encounter one of the innumerable instances of spontaneous telepathic rapport, various examples of which are reported in the literature of parapsychology. They were already observed in antiquity and gave the Stoic philosophers reason to speak of *sympathy*, (*sum* = together + *patheia* = suffering) or co-feeling.

We know from the writings of the mesmerists of the late eighteenth and early nineteenth centuries that they were able to observe these rapport phenomena in their somnambulists under more or less ex-

perimental conditions. These rapport phenomena attracted Schopenhauer's attention. He remarked that this contact which the somnambulists could establish with certain persons differed greatly from the
contacts we have with others in a waking state. While the somnambulists, says Schopenhauer, have no access to any impression through
their own sense organs (anaesthesia[1]), they seem to be able to perceive through the sense organs of their magnetizer.[2] They sneeze,
for example, when he takes snuff, taste and can readily identify what
he eats, and can even hear music heard by the magnetizer although
he may be in an entirely different room. A somnambulist once put
it this way to de Lutzelbourg: "We form only one personality."

By way of amplifying the foregoing in order to gain a better
overall understanding, let us refer to a spontaneous telepathic experience of Dr. Gerda Walther,[3] who is mentioned in my *Magnetiseurs, somnambules en gebedsgenezers*, pages 101 ff., and in the
German edition *Aussergewöhnliche Heilkrafte*, pages 108 ff. One
day in Nuremburg, while listening to a radio broadcast of "Die
Meistersinger" and greatly enjoying the artistry of the famous opera
singer Rode as he interpreted the role of Hans Sachs, Doctor Walther
spontaneously felt that she was getting into telepathic contact with
one of her acquaintances who, it turned out later, was also listening
to this radio broadcast in Munich. Unlike Doctor Walther, however,
he didn't enjoy the broadcast at all and, as he told her later, kept
thinking, "How boring! How long will this last? How I wish it
were over!" Doctor Walther said, "In this way I heard the same
music twice simultaneously: once as myself, delighted with its beauty
and appreciating each word, but beside that, though, as R. S. (the
acquaintance with whom she was spontaneously in telepathic rapport), with little understanding or feeling for the work, and thus as
somebody who was bored."

From information furnished to me by Doctor Walther, it was
apparent that she repeatedly had such experiences with persons
with whom she was on more or less closely affectionate terms. Furthermore, because of her strongly developed sense of discrimination
and her schooling in phenomenology, she knew how to determine in
many cases with just which of her friends and acquaintances she was
experiencing this *Persönlichkeitserweiterung um das Du* ("widening
of personality to include thee as well as me").

Nowadays, psychoscopists furnish us with opportunities to observe the phenomenon of "co-feeling" under experimental conditions. Those of us who have had such subjects under observation have always been impressed by the fact that under certain circumstances they seem to constitute a oneness with their consultants, or with the person for whom the experimenter has handed them an inductor. If this person suffers from one or another ailment, the psychoscopist suffers with him. In the same way as he can think, feel, and will with him; co-suffering, co-thinking, co-feeling and co-willing. Furthermore, we have often had the opportunity of observing that our subjects display a (panto-) mimicry, having a striking, often startling resemblance to those with whom they seem to be in interpsychic contact in telepathic rapport. It is as if they more or less *become* the other person.

The following case will serve as an illustration. It is derived from a session held in 1922 with Mrs. Akkeringa, who was a very well-known psychoscopist in those days, under the auspices of the Dutch Society for Psychical Research. A glove served as an inductor. It belonged to a young girl of 19 who was not personally present at the sitting. This inductor was brought by Mr. L. R., who was among those present at the session and who commented afterwards on the details given by the subject, which had been recorded very accurately.

Words of the psychoscopist	*Comments by Mr. L. R.*
1. Subject folds the glove and then says, "Belongs to someone still alive, not in this room."	The owner of the glove is a 19-year-old girl, staying with strangers.
2. Subject waves the glove around playfully. "I want so very much to sing a song, a children's poem: 'See the moon shining through the trees.' This person has a great love for children."	For her age, she is exceptionally childish and sings a lot. Asked if she prefers to sing a particular song, she answers: "See the moon shining through the trees."
3. Subject pushes her chair a little away from the table. "I belong with the company and yet I like to withdraw a little. This way I'll live my own life—still, everything interests me though."	She is shy, withdraws more or less. When Mrs. V. S., one of those present, saw the girl in a group a few days later, they all sat around the table but her chair was backed away a little bit, exactly as Mrs. Akkeringa had shown.

4. Did she work a lot in the kitchen? (L. R. "No.") I would like to bake things, tarts, something tasty. She must like those things.

In the family she lives with now, she does not help with the household chores. When asked what she preferred to do in her own home, however, she replied, "I like best being busy in the kitchen, baking raisin-cakes and such things."

5. She apparently can be very outspoken, yet she is reserved — a complicated character, not so easy to understand.

She would like to be open, but by nature she is withdrawn. She recognizes she is not as open as she wishes she were.

6. She should be set straight, however, concerning her neatness.

In her present environment she is not untidy or disorderly, but "mother never found her neat enough."

7. Is she going back and forth by train every day? I don't mean on the city tram as here (in Amsterdam) but real country.

She does not travel much but in her thoughts she is always on a journey. To sit in a train is, as it were, an everyday game with her. People around her know this and ask jokingly, for instance, when she sits dreaming, "Where are you going now?"

8. Subject rubs her knees suddenly. What is happening? I have the feeling that both legs are gone and as if I lost all my bearings. Subject feels her hair. As if I have been picked up, knocked down, or fallen off somewhere. It is an awful feeling. No train, tram, but something going past very fast. It is as if it picks me up.

About a year ago she fell off her bike, and hurt her knees. This fall was not at all serious, but caused quite disproportionate emotions. She spoke about it quite often to her roommates and made such a to-do about it; she would always complain about the pain in her knees.

It is not necessary for us to determine on the grounds of their overt behavior alone that they "feel as one" (identify), because their self-observations also give us cause to speak with Marcinowski of *Persönlichkeitserweiterung um das Du* or with Szántó of *eine teilweise Aufgabe der eigenen Zentrierung, um in den Kreis eines fremden Zentrums dringen zu können* ("a partial relinquishment of one's own personality in order to penetrate the center of another person"). It is apparent from various data of an introspective nature which we obtain from our subjects. We observed one of these instances earlier in Chapter II. I'll follow it up with a second example. This one comes from the French paragnost R. de Fleurière, who was one of Doctor Osty's group of subjects. This paragnost told Doctor Osty the following:

Sometimes I have the feeling that the person who consults me *invades* me and that in every aspect I perceive, think, and feel as he does. At other times, I feel as if I am invading my visitor. This experience often reminds me of the striking and significant remark by Mme de Sévigné[4] to her daughter who was troubled by a severe and painful cough: "My daughter, your chest hurts me." Because, thanks to this displacement of my being in his, I can feel his pains with him. It is rather like having at one and the same moment the power to be myself and at the same time a totally strange personality.

Such identifications by psychoscopists are concerned not only with the present, but also the future and the past of their consultants. Osty reported that during a consultation, one of his subjects began to weep copiously and blow her nose continuously. According to the subject, her consultant, who was suffering from an eye disease and was not personally present at the session, and concerning whom she had been able to furnish a few exact data regarding his *status praesens*, would have to expect a similar almost uncontrollable flow of tears in the future. "This, however, will stop suddenly," she went on to say. "It is as if someone with a magic wand makes these symptoms disappear." A few years after this consultation one of the consultant's eyes suddenly began to water. It did not seem very serious at first, but gradually the flood of tears became greater and greater, and there was nothing left for him to do except wipe his face all day and blow his nose continuously besides. The aid of several doctors was sought. None seemed able to alleviate this troublesome and depressing symptom. When the need reached its peak a doctor was consulted who gave the patient several injections of a calcium chloride preparation. From the first injection the flood of tears stopped, and soon the patient was wholly cured, as the subject had predicted.

As evidenced in my own publications, I have been able to observe similar identifications repeatedly in my subjects.[5] That they were already known in Biblical times is illustrated in the Acts of the Apostles 21:10 ff., regarding the prophet Agabus.

In contrast to proscopic identifications are retroscopic (paranormal) identifications, as we have already learned from the report of the testing done with Mrs. Akkeringa. Did not this psychoscopist experience the pains felt a year earlier by the 19-year-old girl when she fell from her bike? We who have observed psychoscopists know that they often display reactualizations of the past.

We have now to establish the remarkable fact that similar reactualizations of the past are not limited to the living but occur also in relation to the dead. With this we approach the subject of spiritism.

Spiritism

By the term spiritism, we understand the belief in a personal survival after death, together with the conviction that under certain circumstances, the dead can come in contact with their earthly survivors.

The principal tenets on which the spiritistic "faith" rests, though, are possession and seeing ghosts. We find such phenomena reported throughout the ages.[6]

Possession

As far as being possessed is concerned, there can be no doubt at all that many cases which may be classified under this heading should be looked at in the light of psychoanalysis, as will be developed further in Chapter V. There are, however, also cases where we obviously have to do with parapsychological phenomena. As has been said earlier, the reactualizations are not limited to the living, but seem to appear also in regard to the dead. During one test of a series taken with a psychoscopist under my supervision, there developed a realistic impersonation of the death-struggle of a businessman, who years before ended his life by taking poison. The subject had never met the businessman during his life, and she had of course been kept in complete ignorance of the origin of the inductor. This was a letter the dead man wrote quite some time before his death; it dealt with a business matter.

On the occasion of another sitting with this subject, she identified herself with a man who had lost his life 68 years earlier by strangulation. She began to behave like somebody being strangled with a cord. Her face twitched like someone who was about to choke and she uttered sounds as if she really was about to choke. Her behavior was so emotionally upsetting that one of the persons present could no longer watch it and had to leave the room. The subject was preoccupied for quite some time—more than an hour— with the impression of what she experienced.[7]

Although such displacements into the past of the dead or the living are not easy to explain, this as I see it is no reason just to reach out for the spiritistic hypothesis. It is quite understandable, though, that some people, having witnessed experiments in which a psychoscopist portrays the conduct of a dead person in a manner suggesting telepathic rapport, will speak of possession in a spiritistic sense.

It has been found that a number of subjects are also inclined to speak on occasion as if they feel that they are possessed in the spiritistic sense, and the dead person revealed through them. I think here, for instance, of Mr. Delta, one of my subjects who repeatedly succeeded in locating the bodies of lost or dead people. In my *Beschouwingen over het gebruik van paragnosten*, pages 110 ff., I reported one or another thing about his performances.

In contrast with Mr. Alpha, mentioned in the same work, pages 28 ff., who in a considerable number of cases can be consulted by telephone, Mr. Delta almost always tries very hard to visit the home of the lost or deceased. Usually, on his arrival there, he first "sees" an apparition of the lost or deceased person. Similar apparitions (often based on an unconscious telepathic influencing by members of the family or neighbors) are followed by a condition of being possessed, in which, much as in telepathic rapport, he is simultaneously himself as well as the other person.

For example, in the case of a man missing at Nijkerk, he felt that he was himself and at the same time also a senile old man, the one who was lost.

To gain a better understanding of what we have written, the conclusion cited earlier by Fleurière is pointed out. Like Fleurière's ability to be at the same time himself and a consultant, whether present or not, Mr. Delta and many other psychoscopists exhibit the power to be simultaneously themselves and the deceased.

Mr. Delta has told me that in such cases of being possessed he has always found it difficult to remain himself, and he is always plagued during experiments with the fear of being completely overpowered by the "other one."

Now we encounter this "overpowering" among a number of so-called trance mediums. Some of these mediums have become great celebrities. Mrs. E. Piper is one of these; an outline of her life is given in my book, *Het Spiritisme*, Chapter XI. Various noted scholars and scientists held seances with her over an extended period of years from 1885 on. From these, it became apparent that she was not only a most remarkable medium, but also at the same time a wholly integrated character, who gladly and without reservations made herself available to those carrying on parapsychological research.

Mrs. Piper was a so-called trance-medium, that is, a subject who enters a kind of "somnambulistic" or auto hypnotic state. In this state, she impressed those present as a woman possessed by strange entities who used her speech organs (so-called automatic speech) and her hands also (so-called automatic writing). In a number of cases, the entities that spoke and wrote "through" her were unmistakably products of the so-called dramatic splitting of personality, thus so-called secondary and tertiary personalities. It cannot be denied that in these personalities the medium repeatedly demonstrated most remarkable paragnostic gifts. There were also entities, however, which "manifested themselves" through her whose nature aroused controversy. Rightly or wrongly, some researchers could not abandon the conviction that she sometimes came into telepathic rapport with a deceased person, who tried to establish his identity by bringing up all sorts of old memories (often in connection with all kinds of "trivialities").[8] In those seances it was as if, to a certain degree, the medium possessed the memory of the deceased one. The secondary and tertiary personalities sometimes also seemed to possess remarkable knowledge about events which had occurred in the past of deceased people.

The following example, taken from one of the numerous seance reports on Mrs. Piper made by the English scientist Sir Oliver Lodge, will serve as an illustration. Sir Oliver had an Uncle Robert in London, who was already a very old man at the time the sittings were held. This uncle, a brother of Sir Oliver's deceased father, had had a twin brother who had died more than twenty years earlier. The researcher asked his uncle to send him some relic or other of that deceased twin brother. Not long afterwards Lodge received in the mail a gold watch, worn by the deceased brother, and to which he was strongly attached. That same day, in turn, Lodge handed the watch to Mrs. Piper, who was in a state of trance. "Phinuit," one of this medium's secondary personalities, who claimed to be a deceased French doctor and who appeared as her so-called "spiritual amanuensis" (a guardian spirit or so-called "control"),[9] reported almost immediately to Sir Oliver that the watch had belonged to one of his uncles, whose death from a fall had been mentioned earlier. According to Phinuit, this uncle was extremely fond of Uncle Robert, who had sent the consultant the watch. With great difficulty Phinuit succeeded in giving the name of the deceased twin brother as Jerry (short for Jeremiah). After that, Phinuit reported that Jerry was personally present and would like to give some messages. Then the medium (speaking as under the influence of the deceased owner of the inductor) said, "This is my watch and Robert is my brother, and I myself am here."

Lodge now began to explain to "Jerry" that he could only deliver proof of his presence by succeeding in bringing up all sorts of minor particulars—those known only to him and his brother Robert—about his childhood. In subsequent seances a few details of this kind were given.

According to Lodge, Uncle Jerry,

> ... recalled episodes such as swimming the creek when they were boys together, and running some risk of getting drowned; killing a cat in Smith's field; the possession of a small rifle, and of a long peculiar skin, like a snakeskin, which he thought was now in the possession of Uncle Robert.
>
> All these facts have been more or less completely verified. But the interesting thing is that his twin brother, from whom I got the watch, and with whom I was thus in a sort of communication, could not remember them all. He recollected something about swimming the creek, though he himself had merely looked on. He had a distinct recollection of having had the snakeskin, and of the box in which it was kept, though he does not recall Smith's field. His memory, however, is decidedly failing him, and he was good enough to write to another brother, Frank, living in Cornwall, an old sea captain, and ask if he had any better remembrance of certain facts—of course, not giving any inexplicable reasons for asking. The result of this inquiry was triumphantly to vindicate the existence of Smith's field as a place

near their home, where they used to play, in Barking, Essex; and the
killing of a cat by another brother was also recollected, while of the
swimming of the creek, near a mill-race, full details were given, Frank
and Jerry being the heroes of that foolhardy episode....

Without in any way denying that we have here details which, considered along with the results of innumerable sittings held with Mrs.
Piper over the course of years, furnish unmistakable proof of the
remarkable paragnostic gifts for which Mrs. Piper was renowned
over several decades, still by no means do we see in these and similar
details any proof in the strictly scientific manner of the correctness of
the spiritistic faith. For there always remains the possibility that the
medium achieved a telepathic relationship with the psyches of the
two brothers, Robert and Frank, and that her knowledge was consequently derived in a paranormal way from the psyches of these two
still-living persons. The thesis can also be propounded that, if we
accept the idea that every human in his "deepest being" knows his
own destiny, the subject then could have borrowed her knowledge
of the forthcoming memory from Sir Oliver himself (precognitive
telepathy). For shortly after the session, was he not informed of the
contents of the correspondence between his two uncles?

A few researchers have attempted, with the help of the "cosmic
reservoir" hypothesis and/or so-called clairvoyance in the past, to
explain the most remarkable fact that people like Mrs. Piper are
able to "bring to mind" (inneren) under certain circumstances what
the deceased could remember during their earthly existence. It is
to the credit of philosophers like F. Ortt and J. M. J. Kooy that their
speculations, based on the theories of Minkowski, Einstein, and others,
have given some content and meaning to these vague conceptions.
Briefly, their speculations amount to this: under certain circumstances,
paragnosts might be able to follow the four-dimensional "time-lines"
or "trajectories" in a paranormal way and thereby, as it were, move
in the second dimension of time, or in the sphere of eternity as well
(Ortt).[10]

Although I can see in speculations of this kind no more than the
first meritorious attempts to show that retroscopic as well as proscopic
phenomena are less incomprehensible in the light of modern philosophy than many would suppose, it should be mentioned nevertheless

that there have also been statements by paragnosts suggesting that there are some kernels of truth in such speculations. Here, for instance, I think of the theosophist seer C. W. Leadbeater, whose writings undeniably have a certain heuristic value. In his book, *Man: Whence, How, and Whither?*, coauthored by Annie Besant, he writes that the clairvoyant can survey the past as well as identify with persons chosen at random who lived in the past. According to Leadbeater and others, these phenomena depend on identifications similar to those which cause us to speak of being possessed and retroscopic telepathic rapport (retroscopic paranormal identification).

The next case to follow should provide a better understanding of the above. It concerns a Sra. Maria Reyes de Z., a very intelligent Mexican woman who served for a considerable time as a subject for the German doctor, G. Pagenstecher, who resided in Mexico for many years. She is generally recognized to be one of the most gifted psychoscopists mentioned in the literature of parapsychology.

On March 30, 1921, after he had placed her under hypnosis, Doctor Pagenstecher handed Sra. Reyes de Z. a sealed envelope obviously containing a letter. Its contents were unknown to the experimenter, who had received it through an attorney as intermediary. After the subject had achieved her usual visionary state, she related that she felt as if she was aboard a great steamship. Although the sea was calm, the passengers around her moved in a state of great excitement. Several of them paced the deck despairingly. Some of them donned life jackets. Just in front of her she saw a large, rather corpulent man with a pale complexion, great dark eyes, black hair and eyebrows. His forehead was broad, he had an aquiline nose and a full beard and moustache. She judged his age to be about 40. He was a true Spanish type. Over his left eye she saw a broad scar. The psychoscopist then described how she saw the man tear a page out of a notebook and write a few lines on it with a pencil, using a cabin wall to lean on. Several violent explosions followed right after that. The man stopped writing for a moment, then added a few more words. Next, the subject saw him roll up the paper and put it in a bottle, which he closed by ramming its cork firmly against the cabin wall. Finally, he threw the bottle overboard. Then the explosions became still more violent, and the ship began to sink. She then heard the Spaniard cry out: "¡Dios mio, mis hijos!" ("My God, my children!") During as well as after this vision, the subject moved in a markedly agitated way. Her entire body trembled. When she awoke from her hypnotic state, she furnished a number of closer details. Among other things, she said that the shipwrecked man's scar showed over his right and not his left eye, as she had said initially.

When a second sealed envelope belonging with the inductor, after inspection to make certain that all of the seals were unbroken, was opened in the presence of four witnesses, including the American researcher Dr. Walter Prince, it was learned that the inductor contained a torn scrap of paper on which had been written in Spanish: "The ship sinks. Good-bye, my Luisa. Take care of my children and see that they won't forget me." A postscript followed: "Habana. May God protect you and me. Good-bye."

In a letter that accompanied the inductor, and which also reached Doctor Pagenstecher through an attorney, as intermediary, we read that Mr. J. W. H. was a very well-known businessman, who had been a friend of Doctor Pagenstecher's for years. Mr. J. W. H. became acquainted with a lady whose husband had died, in all probability, on May 7, 1915. He was a passenger on the *Lusitania*, the ship that was sunk by a German submarine as it is assumed everybody knows.

The letter in the sealed envelope which served as an inductor was washed ashore in a bottle some time after the sinking of the *Lusitania* and after some meandering reached Havana. Because of a strong supposition that the letter came from a Spaniard named Ramon Penoles, Sra. Penoles obtained it, as she had sound reasons to assume that her husband had lost his life in the *Lusitania* disaster. Among other things in the note that accompanied the inductor were given a description of Ramon Penoles. When this description is compared with the one given by the psychoscopist about the passenger she saw, it can only be admitted that her description was a "perfect hit." Ramon Penoles was 38 years old and left two children, a boy 5 and a girl 3 years old.

Although we cannot state positively that this is a case of so-called clairvoyance in the past, we must nevertheless take this possibility into account.[11] One of the arguments which can be advanced in favor of the hypothesis of retroscopy is that the subject *felt* as if she was aboard the doomed ship. Now, a similar "living in the midst of events of the past" is regarded by Leadbeater and others as one of the features of a sure "look back" (retroscopy). According to him and others, the clairvoyant places himself in the "still present" past, a statement which is much less fantastic in view of the time-orbits theories of Ortt, Kooy and others than it may seem to many.*

According to Leadbeater and others, there is now also a possibility for the clairvoyant to identify himself with certain figures in such displacements to the past. This would mean, then, that the possibility existed for Sra. Reyes de Z. to experience something like a retroscopic telepathic rapport phenomenon in relation to Ramon Penoles, in which case it must have seemed to those present at the seance that she was possessed by the spirit of the deceased.

Seeing Ghosts

What applies to the so-called cases of "being possessed" applies also to many cases of seeing ghosts. These also can be explained as animistic, so-called, with the help of the psychic powers or capacities present in living man, as I showed in my *Het Spiritisme*, Chapter VI. Although I dwelt at some length on seeing ghosts in that book, a short explanation of this phenomenon will not be out of place here.

First, I'll take a case of spontaneous telepathy which I reported previously in my *Inleiding tot de parapsychologie*, page 64. It concerns a psychiatrist who, during a psychoanalytical session with a Mr. Z., suddenly had a pseudo-hallucinatory experience concerning a silk cap with a black silk peak. The doctor correctly connected this experience with one or another suppressed emotional event in the life of his patient. Later it seemed to him this vision was correct. The patient told him that his father, with whom he could not get along,

---

* Those familiar with the writings of the theosophist "seers" know that they mention indelible picture-like traces left in a super-material substance by everything that happens. This super-material substance is frequently called by the Sanskrit term *Akasha*. The Akashic Record is seen as a sort of superindividual All-memory.

did wear such a cap. A series of details followed afterwards about unpleasant experiences, which the patient had suppressed, associated with this cap.

It is obvious that instead of the cap (a father attribute) an image of the father himself could have appeared to the doctor. For parapsychological research has demonstrated that similar visions are by no means necessarily limited to attributes.

Now, if the doctor in this case had had a vision of the father of the patient, there would be two possibilities, that is to say, either the father was still alive (in which case we would have a *phantasm* of a living person, originating in the unconscious and involuntary telepathic influence from a third party), or the father had died a long or short time ago. In the second case, we would have to call this a phantasm of a dead person. This phantasm of a dead person must, then, have had its origin in the psyche of a living one (the son), and consequently must be explained as animistic and not spiritistic. Similar ghost-apparitions to be explained animistically now occur frequently with psychoscopists.

The cases are numerous in which psychoscopists, as a result of an unconscious and involuntary telepathic influence from their consultants, can describe persons with whom the consultants have been in contact in the past. It does not ordinarily make any difference whether the image seen and described by the psychoscopist involves a person still living or someone who may have died.* Nevertheless, a lot of them seem to show an inclination to claim incorrectly that images associated with deceased persons are ghost-apparitions in the spiritistic sense. It seems to happen again and again that psychoscopists wrongly suppose apparitions of living persons to be apparitions of the deceased. Thus, for example, a psychoscopist described the image of an old man sitting in a wheelchair to a lady whom she did not know. The psychoscopist thought she was describing the dead father of the consultant, who was trying to give proof of his presence and survival after death through the psychoscopist. The consultant could only answer that, although the description was correct, the

---

* As an example, I refer to the vision described by Mr. Eta of the "young man with the crooked back, who cursed horribly" (see Chapter III).

interpretation was not, because her father was still very much alive. The apparition of the aged and obviously ill man had suggested to the psychoscopist, or made her conclude incorrectly, that she saw a ghost-apparition.

One should not assume from the foregoing that I am opposed to the possibility that there may be apparitions which originate in a telepathic influence from the deceased. Personally, I am not unwilling to take this possibility into consideration, although it should be admitted that, until now, scientific parapsychological proof that human personality survives death has not been established. As yet, the spiritistic hypothesis is an open question in parapsychology.

The opinion that an important part of the apparitions of living and deceased persons should be regarded as veridical pseudo-hallucinations, which in most cases are based on an unconscious and involuntary telepathic influence by the living—and possibly but by no means certainly also by the dead in exceptional cases—clarifies much that previously had seemed inexplicable. For one thing, apparitions of the living, dying and dead that have been mentioned periodically through the ages are always clothed. Often they also carry various objects with them. Thus, for example, in *Phantasms of the Living*, Case No. 212,[12] we find the report of one Doctor Bowstead. He was playing cricket one morning and went after a ball he had missed and which had rolled under a hedge, when suddenly his half brother appeared, dressed in hunting costume with a gun under his arm. It turned out later that at that moment, when about to leave the house dressed in hunting clothes and with his gun, this half brother had suddenly died.

This complicated case, like countless analogous instances mentioned in publications concerned with spontaneous telepathy, strengthens our conviction that most, at least, if not all apparitions have no material basis whatsoever, but must be regarded as pure pseudo-hallucinations and hallucinations which, however—and this is very important—differ from the hallucinations of the mentally ill by their veridical character, among other things.[13]

In psychology we learn that hallucinations show a certain kinship to dream-images. On the basis of this similarity, we should expect that certain characteristics which are quite common in dream-images would also occur in hallucinations. Cases reported by several researchers will not disappoint us in this expectation.

We have first of all the fact that dreams as we know often carry an allegorical character, which is consistent with a lowering of the level of consciousness, characteristic of sleep. In this state, an archaic tendency to think in images is revived.

Now this allegorical character is also found in a number of apparitions. For instance, Mr. J. N. S. reported that at the moment his friend and colleague F. L. *quite suddenly* died of a rupture of the aorta, he saw him appear in his living room with a hat with a black mourning band. The apparition also wore a loosely buttoned overcoat and had a walking stick in his hand. Since an investigation disclosed that Mr. F. L. actually had died in bed in his nightclothes, there is every reason to believe that we must regard this hat with the mourning band and the other attributes of this apparition as allegorical representations of his dying. Hat and outerwear must be seen here unmistakably as products of the archaic inclination to think in images, which we have already learned from dream research.

With the so-called *Verbildlichung* ("transformation of images") characteristic of dreams are associated so-called *condensation* (pressing together) and *displacement*. Both are also characteristic of the hallucinations produced by telepathic influence.

As an example of displacement, the reported case of the cap can again be cited. Instead of a frightened image of a feared father, that of his cap appears (an image associated with that of the father and with which are associated unpleasant feelings). There are further fine examples of displacement in my *Het Spiritisme*, Chapter VI.

In the same chapter of that book, I reported a clear example of condensation (pressing together). It concerns Mrs. W. of Bussum who, when a friend who lived in Brussels died unexpectedly one night, saw her appear. Because in this case the vision not only announced the death but also contained in allegorical form a prediction regarding an inheritance, there is every reason to speak here of condensation.

The next case can also serve as an example of pressing together. It concerns Frau X. She resided with her husband in a small town in Bavaria more than 300 kilometers from her birthplace, a small Swiss town where her mother lived and from whom she received letters from time to time. At the time of her nocturnal vision, she was aware of no reason at all to be anxious about her mother.

In a state between sleeping and waking one morning she had a vision which had the quality of a nightmare. In it, she saw herself taking a stroll along the shore of a familiar lake. She walked very peacefully, as she had done so often there during her childhood. She watched the fish swimming in the transparent water. At the bottom of the lake, she noticed a sewer pipe which emptied itself into it. Suddenly, she saw an arm emerge from the water, not far from the shore. The hand held a letter, more precisely an ordinary-sized envelope, and the hand seemed to want to show her the letter. For a moment the arm moved through the water in the same direction she was going, and then the arm disappeared beneath the water.

Although this vision depressed her very much, she could find no explanation for it. In the course of the day, however, she received a telegram from her family in Switzerland, requesting her to come immediately because her mother had become very ill. Then she started to look for a connection between the dream-vision and the telegram, without finding any. Circumstances prevented her from going to her mother in Switzerland, and thus she had to wait for the letter promised in the telegram. It brought the explanation for her dream. Plagued by deep sorrow, her mother had apparently drowned herself in the lake after writing a farewell note giving the motivating cause of her act of despair. This letter was found in a table drawer. The corpse was found not far from shore. The day and hour of the suicide matched the time of the nocturnal vision. Witnesses confirmed the accuracy of the report.

In this vision also, it is possible to see an example of condensation because several images were compressed into one.

Until now we have paid attention only to apparitions involving people to whom they were somehow related.

Research into spontaneous paragnosis has disclosed that visions of people appear occasionally to people who don't have any connection with the subject of the "hallucinating." Thus, a Mrs. Z. reported that once, when she spent the night in a boarding house in Cheltenham, she woke up without any seeming reason and to her surprise saw an old man with a round, ruddy face standing at the foot of her bed. He was dressed in an old-fashioned blue coat, with brass buttons, a light-colored vest and a pair of full trousers. The more she looked at him, the clearer she saw every line and detail of his attire. Although she could take all this in so accurately, she remained aware that the old gentleman was not really there; thus, the term pseudo-hallucination is used in this case. She closed her eyes after a while, and when she reopened them, the apparition was gone. Her investigation revealed that she had seen an apparition of an earlier inhabitant of the house, quite unknown to her, who had died some time ago.

Many people think that such cases are hard to explain in any other than a spiritistic way. That this opinion is open to doubt can be demonstrated by the fact that such phenomena are also known to occur in cases of former inhabitants who were found upon inquiry to be still alive. I mentioned an example of such a case in *Tijdschrift voor parapsychologie* XX, page 182. It concerned one of my subjects. One day he touched the doorknob of a room in a house he visited for the first time, when suddenly the image of an old woman appeared before him. She hobbled through the room on a crutch. He "saw" the furniture change, also. None of those present could identify the image. At the request of the paragnost, the neighbors were consulted. It then appeared that he had given a detailed description of a still-living earlier occupant of this house and her surroundings.[14]

It also seems to happen that subjects see images, spontaneous or not, of future occupants of a house. Thus, I witnessed the subject Gamma "seeing" a child about three years old walking through the living room in the house of a couple of middle-aged married friends of mine. More than four years later, that "seen" child—still unborn at the time of the prediction—lived for some time with them. It was brought into the world by their niece. Through a combination of circumstances, this couple had the child literally inflicted upon them. I am in a position to affirm, because I know all of the facts in this matter, that it is impossible to consider the prediction, in this case, as a cause for the event which took place later.[15]

If we return now to the case reported by Mrs. Z. about the apparition in a boarding house at Cheltenham, it is to point out that such a case can also serve as a good example of local spook-apparitions. In her well-documented book[16] about this and related subjects, Fanny Moser correctly pointed out that the existence of such phenomena becomes ever more difficult to deny. C. G. Jung, who supplied her book with a foreword, told us rightly that one of the future tasks of psychology will be to solve the problems which these phenomena place before us.

Chapter V

REINCARNATION

(memories and supposed memories of past lives)

"Sensation du deja vu" and Belief in Reincarnation

WILLEM KLOOS, in one of his *Binnengedachten* ("Inner Thoughts") (No. 399, *De Nieuwe Gids*, Dec. 1928) recounted that when visiting South German cities, he sometimes had an overpowering feeling that he had lived in them in a previous existence. Wrongly, they seemed to him to be somehow familiar.[1]

That Kloos is not the only one who has been inclined to believe in reincarnation because of a "sensation du déjà vu" is evident from the statements of several well-known authors, among them Charles Dickens and Alfred M. Lamartine.

The first-mentioned wrote the following in his *Pictures from Italy*:

> At sunset, when I was walking on alone, while the horses rested, I arrived upon a little scene, which, by one of those singular mental operations of which we are all conscious, seemed perfectly familiar to me, and which I see distinctly now. There was not much in it. In the blood-red light, there was a mournful sheet of water, just stirred by the evening wind; upon its margin a few trees. In the foreground was a group of silent peasant-girls leaning over the parapet of a little bridge, and looking, now up at the sky, now down into the water; in the distance, a deep bell; the shadow of approaching night on everything. If I had been murdered there, in some former life, I could not have seemed to remember the place more thoroughly, or with a more emphatic chilling of the blood; and the real remembrance of it acquired in that minute, is so strengthened by the imaginary recollection, that I hardly think I could forget it.[2]

And we read the following in Lamartine's *Voyage en Orient*:

> In Judea I had neither bible nor guidebook in my hand, nor anyone to tell me the names of the ancient valleys and mountains. Yet I clearly recognized the valley of Féré, Cinthe, and the battle-

[88]

field of Saul. . the next morning at the foot of a barren mountain I recognized the grave of the Maccabees. . . Except for the valleys of Lebanon, I have almost never encountered a place or a thing in Judea which did not seem to me like a memory. Have we, then, lived twice, or a thousand times?

It ought to be evident from the discussions of "sensation du déjà vu" in Chapters I and III that it is wholly premature to surmise that one has previously inhabited another earthly body simply on the strength of such a sensation. We have already shown that there are available easier and simpler explanations for such experiences. As long as we are not absolutely certain that a case under discussion cannot possibly be explained in terms of accepted hypotheses, it is scientifically irresponsible to take refuge in the hypothesis of reincarnation—even though this belief in reembodiment has been held from remotest antiquity down to our time.[3]

The Reincarnation Fantasies of Helene Smith

In the year 1894 Prof. Théodore Flournoy of Geneva became acquainted with Hélène Müller, who was then unmarried and about 40.[4] She was employed by a large business firm in Geneva and enjoyed the absolute confidence of the management, who regarded her highly because of her trustworthiness and great devotion to her duties.

Flournoy described her as a well-educated woman with interests in art and literature. As a child, Flournoy was told, Hélène was "a bit different from the others." She was withdrawn, avoided playing with her friends, and would sometimes sit motionless for half an hour at a time, falling into various day dreams in which she had visions of all sorts of colors, landscapes, and ruins. Upon attaining the age of about 14, she began getting a variety of nocturnal fantasies. Often, her dream-images became (pseudo-)hallucinatory experiences. In the year 1892 Hélène became associated with spiritists. She was introduced into a séance group by a girlfriend. Quite soon, she revealed herself as a medium, heard "voices," saw spirits, and began automatic writing.

One day a "spirit," which up until then had not manifested itself, "appeared" to the group to which Hélène belonged. He said that his task was to act as the spirit guide of the medium. When asked his name, he replied that he was the French poet Victor Hugo! For several days Hélène was deeply impressed by this manifestation, which persisted for several months. "Victor Hugo" gave her fatherly advice and also wrote a few poems through her hand (automatic writing).[5]

After several months a "spirit" calling himself "Leopold" arrived. He was to become thenceforth her inseparable companion for the years following. "Victor Hugo" now withdrew. Hélène described "Leopold" as about 35 years old, attired in black. He showed assurance from the beginning and declared he had a better right to act as her spirit guide than "Victor Hugo" did, because he had already known Hélène in one of their previous incarnations.

Difficult as it was for Hèlène to say goodbye to "Victor Hugo" and accept "Leopold" in his place, she nevertheless had to put up with this turn of events because the manifestations of "Victor Hugo" were becoming less and less frequent and those of "Leopold" increasingly so. The medium's reluctance to accept "Leopold" stemmed in part from the fact that he did not seem to have any antecedents. Her vanity had been gratified greatly by having been chosen as a medium by "Victor Hugo."

One day Hélène saw "Leopold" appear before her with a carafe in his hand. When she told the others present at the séance what she saw, one of them remarked that this reminded her of a passage in Chapter XV of Alexandre Dumas' *Mémoires d'un médecin, Joseph Balsamo*, where Balsamo—the real name of the notorious Count Cagliostro—is pictured with a carafe and a wand.

The visitor wondered whether Balsamo and "Leopold" might possibly be one and the same person. She talked about this after the séance with Hélène and showed her the picture in an illustrated edition of Dumas' works.

What might have been expected happened. At a séance soon afterwards, the message was obtained by means of table-tipping that "Leopold" once, on earth, bore the name Giuseppe Balsamo. From then on, the medium accepted him completely.[6]

Hélène adhered to a belief in reincarnation, and "Leopold" claimed to have become acquainted with her in one of their previous incarnations. This, of course, raised the question of who Hélène had been at that time. "Leopold" claimed he had known her while he was still Cagliostro. Possibly then she was Lorenza Feliciani?

This notion of her fanciful admirer—the same one who had also suggested that "Leopold" and Cagliostro were presumably one and the same person—made a deep impression on the medium. She soon declared that she had been Lorenza Feliciani in a previous incarnation and had known "Leopold" *alias* Cagliostro during that earthly existence.

One day Hélène was shocked to discover that Lorenza Feliciani was only a figment of Alexandre Dumas' imagination and could not be regarded as a real historical figure. Not long after this disappointing discovery, a message was received saying that Hélène was a reincarnation of the French Queen Marie Antoinette.

Flournoy supposed that Hélène borrowed the material for her personification of Marie Antoinette from Dumas' writings. He was impressed, nevertheless, with the manner in which she carried off her role of Marie Antoinette: "... Il faut voir, quand la trance royale est franche et complète, la grâce, l'élégance, la distinction, la majesté parfois, qui éclatent dans l'attitude et le geste d'- Hélène. Elle a vraiment un port de reine." The finest variegations in expression: sweet amiability, haughty condescension, pity, indifference, contempt, changed face and bearing as she encountered the imaginary courtiers that peopled her dreams. Her gestures with her handkerchief and with objects conjured up in her imagination: a fan, an eyeglass, a smelling bottle, her bows, never forgetting to sweep back an imaginary train—all totally natural and easy.

Her portrayal of the "royal type," however, representing the ill-fated Austrian wife of Louis XVI, was miserably deficient. The writing Hélène produced in her role of Marie Antoinette bore little or no resemblance to what the French Queen has left to us. Hélène's relationship, in trance, to "Leopold" or Cagliostro, whom she called her "cher sorcier," was of an entirely different character than that painted for us by the historians. According to them, Marie Antoinette harbored only contempt for Cagliostro. And so we could go on reporting points of difference between the real Marie Antoinette and the one Hélène tried to portray in her trance.[7]

Besides a "royal cycle," Flournoy also described a "Hindu period" and, further, a "Martian cycle" experienced by Hélène Smith.

Her "Hindu romance" was an account of what Hélène went through as the daughter of a 14th century Arabian sheikh. She became the eleventh wife of an Indian prince Sivrouka Nayaca and was known as Princess Simandini. Upon the death of her husband, in accordance with the customs of the country, she was immolated on the funeral pyre with his corpse.

In her role as Princess Simandini also, Hélène in trance proved to be an excellent actress who had retained in her memory everything she had ever read about the East and was able to use it in a refined way to make her fabrications a success.

In some respects the Martian cycle is more remarkable than the Hindu romance. In this cycle, she introduced us to the inhabitants of the planet Mars, who described all sorts of things about life on that planet and who through the medium, tried to familiarize those in the circle with the language spoken on this planet. The chapters devoted to this cycle by Flournoy should undoubtedly be regarded as a contribution to our knowledge of *glossolalia.*[8]

Freud opened our eyes to the fact that, under certain conditions, we can suppress the contents of our consciousness. Such suppressed contents of our consciousness are not destroyed. They are banished to the subconscious, where they remain, "go on and on," and try again to push their way through towards the consciousness. Thus, so-called neurotic symptoms originate.

Among other neurotic symptoms are the "wish-dreams." From studying these dreams, we can learn our most secret wishes. We know that in a large number of cases these wishes are revealed only indirectly. Freud says that there is a Censor within us, and consequently many of our wishes show up in symbolic form.

Stekel called attention to the fact that, in our dreams, our most secret wishes are revealed in a very poetic way. He concluded from this not only that a poet lives within each human being, but also that we should regard poetry (or any work of art) as a sort of objectified dream-image. According to him, the poet (novelist, etc.) is a neurotic who has succeeded in objectifying by one means or another his dream-images. "My investigations have brought me positive proof," he wrote in *Dichtung und Neurose* ("Composition and Neurosis"), Wiesbaden, 1909, "that there is no difference at all between a neurotic and a poet. Not every neurotic is a poet, but every poet is a neurotic."

It is noteworthy that long before the arrival of Freud and his school, there were statements by various poets showing that they could be regarded as the forerunners of the psychoanalysts. Goethe, Hawthorne, Heine, and Hebbel belong to this group. The last mentioned wrote in one of his diaries: "Mein Gedanke dass Traum und Poesie identisch sind bestätigt sich nun mehr und mehr." ("My ideas that dream and poetry are identical are increasingly confirmed.") And Grillparzer, who could be counted correctly by Stekel as among the precursors of the psychoanalysts, drew a comparison in his *Abschied aus Gastein* ("Farewell to Gastein") between a pearl and a work of art. "Beide werden erzeugt in Todesnot und Qualen." ("Both are produced in agonizing need and torment.")[9]

Yet more significant than this is the following declaration, also by Grillparzer:

> *Dichten heisst denn freilich eben*
> *Im Fremden Dasein eigne's Leben.*

Grillparzer's meaning is that the poet (a word we should not define too narrowly) as the dreamer tries to live his life in the figures created by himself.

After having compared the contents of Grillparzer's autobiography with the contents of *Der Traum ein Leben* (1931), Stekel shows quite convincingly that the various characters appearing in this work performed deeds for which Grillparzer felt an urge but could not fulfill for one reason or another. "The entire drama," according to Stekel, "is a paraphrase of his neurotic thoughts."

What holds true for Grillparzer holds equally true for countless other poets.[10] They too, like Grillparzer, knew how to overcome, by means of artistic sublimation, the censorship (resistance) to their suppressed ideas, feelings, goals. Because of their success in this, they were protected in a number of instances from "nervous disorders" and crime. It may be asked what might have happened to Grillparzer if this process of sublimation had not been effective. Most likely, he would have become a victim of a serious nervous disorder, or . . . a man who might have tried to kill his father and brother.

We are indebted to Freud for defining sublimation. According to Freud, we are speaking of sublimation when, for example, an artist with an unsatisfying love life creates a figure of a madonna. We may view such a painting or statue as an objectified dream-image, an element of a wish-dream projected into the exterior world as a thing. We also speak of sublimation when a woman with an unsatisfied desire for children assumes the position of mother in an orphanage, or when someone like Schiller, for instance, tries to satisfy his supposed feeling of hatred for his father by writing a play in which a tyrant (father image) is murdered.

As the poet, to a certain extent, can live his life to the full through the figures he creates, so also, under special circumstances and to a certain degree, can the actor live his life to the full by acting out certain characters. According to R. Müller Freienfels, the true art of the theater is not just copying externals, but giving form to something. From the true actor, the semblance of reality of life comes, not from imitating models, but from placing himself inside the skin of another and getting rid of inner tensions by identifying himself with someone else.

A few years ago I became acquainted with a man who worked in a well-known ladies' specialty shop. As a reaction to the ill-treatment he had suffered at the hands of the clientele, this man had recurrent dreams which were as clear as could be. He also had daydreams. Thus he imagined in a daydream that he was a rich Turk and possessed a harem "with about a thousand women" who served him as slaves. Out of curiosity this fellow was attracted to a spiritists' circle, in which quite soon he revealed himself to be a medium. The "spirits" which were said to manifest themselves through him were predominantly warlike figures. One of them, who called himself "the captain," claimed that he had served during his earthly existence under van Heutz and had performed all kinds of heroic deeds in Atjeh, a province in Sumatra. Although what was said was "childish" and trivial, it could not be denied, however, that the mimicry and pantomime of this so-called medium were at times interesting. This is understandable if we bear in mind that, in a state of trance, individuation becomes weaker so that identification (which affords an opportunity to live out one's unconscious tensions) becomes correspondingly easier.[11]

It should be plain from what was set forth previously that the "spirits" which were said to manifest themselves through this medium should be regarded as neurotic symptoms, objectified dream-images. We can view this man, along with many other so-called mediums, in principle as a kind of combination of novelist and actor.

Similarly, the earlier-mentioned Hélène Smith could be regarded as such a combination. While the creation of her "guiding spirit" Leopold is undoubtedly associated[12] with her desire for a protecting husband,[13] it can be said concerning the figures of Marie Antoinette and Princess Simandini that we are concerned here with the acted out dream-images of a woman suffering from megalomania. This megalomania stems from her inability to be satisfied with her humdrum existence as an office worker regardless of the fact that, as such, she was highly regarded by her employers.

The Hypnotic Experiments of A. de Rochas

Prof. A. D. Wiersma, in his *Capita Psychopathologica*,[14] described a young woman of 25 whom he placed under hypnosis, after which by suggestion he could cause her to regress to the age of eight. "It was remarkable how her entire appearance changed. She began to behave like a child of that age; her writing was like that of a young child, and she made appropriate mistakes. She remembered whom she went to school with, and who sat on the next bench."

Similar tests had been undertaken late in the nineteenth century by von Krafft Ebing. There is thus reason to wonder whether, upon being regressed to the age of a child, a subject would behave as he or she actually did at that age, or instead as he might imagine he behaved at that age. If the latter is the case, then we are dealing with tests which differ little or not at all from those in which it is suggested to a subject that he is a chimney sweep or a baker. In such cases, the subject begins to act as he thinks a chimney sweep or a baker would. Richet called this *l'objectivation des types* ("objectification of types.")

The German philosopher Leibniz, who in principle was not opposed to a belief in reincarnation,[15] remarked in his *Nouveaux essais sur l'entendement humain*, through an imaginary character Theophilus, that a "non-material being or spirit cannot be robbed of any perception from his previous existence."

We'll leave it an open question whether the French researcher A. de Rochas was familiar with this declaration, but will simply point out that he proceeded to develop the theme begun by Krafft Ebing and that he tried to regress his subjects back into prenatal stages. Reports on this are found in the second part of his *Les vies successives,* Paris, 1911, to which we will now direct our attention.

Under the influence of mesmeric passes,[16] his subjects, de Rochas writes,

> ...seem to be brought back to earlier periods of their present lives, with the intellectual and physiological details characteristic of those periods, and those to the time of their births.[17] When these mesmeric actions were continued until before birth, without the use of suggestion the subject is made to move through situations which, according to the subject, correspond with previous incarnations, and also through intervals separating incarnations.

The following was extracted from one of de Rochas' case records. It is about Josephine, an 18-year-old girl employed in a tailor shop.

Josephine is "regressed" by de Rochas to the age of seven. She says that she is going to school and is learning to write. Given a pen, she writes the words "papa" and "mama" quite well.

After that, she is "regressed" further. Now she is five years old. She is given a handkerchief with the suggestion that it is a doll. She is very pleased and starts to cuddle the doll. Her behavior makes one think of a child of that age.

Next, de Rochas "regresses" her still further. Now she is a baby in a cradle. When a finger is placed in her mouth, she begins to suck. After a few sessions, de Rochas proceeded to "regress" her by the use of longitudinal passes in order to return her to childhood more quickly. When he now asked her questions, she could only answer in pantomine. In this manner, she "told" him that she was not yet born, that the body in which she was to live was in her mother's abdomen and that she was trying to take possession of that body.

When, after several sessions, de Rochas tried to return her still further, a personality appeared who refused to identify himself. He declared in a rude tone and with a man's voice that he was in the dark and couldn't see a thing. With great difficulty de Rochas was able to establish that he was an old man lying on a bed—a farmer. After struggling for a while he gave his name: Jean Code Bourdon. Finally de Rochas persuaded him to write out his name. Later on, de Rochas dictated this name to Josephine, in a waking state, and compared the two signatures. They showed quite obvious differences. Bourdon gave as his residence the hamlet of Champvent in the commune of Polliat. He could not recall the name of the prefecture. After studying an ordnance map at quite some length, de Rochas finally succeeded in locating this hamlet. The researcher appended a note telling how surprising these communications were to him.

When he asked Josephine in a waking state if she had ever heard of the hamlet of Champvent, she replied in the negative. Bourdon related that he was born in 1812 and gave a description of his life, including various dates. He told about his military service with a regiment at Besançon, and about his debauchery.

He said that he had been an atheist and despised the priests. After his death, his spirit supposedly hovered over the coffin and thus witnessed the funeral. He said he remained at the cemetery with his corpse for a long time, and suffered quite a bit during the process of decomposition. He lived in darkness, a most unpleasant situation for him. But because he had neither stolen nor murdered anyone, he did not suffer greatly. However, he was always thirsty, owing to the fact that he had imbibed too much during his lifetime. Death was entirely different than he had imagined. If he had known beforehand what it would be like, he would not have sneered at the priest.

The darkness in which he was plunged seemed to be transitory. He got the feeling that he would be reincarnated in a woman's body. This because women had to suffer more than men, and he had to do penance for his misdeeds in seducing a number of women and abusing them sexually. He chose as his mother someone pregnant with a child of the female sex and gradually forced himself into the body of this child. Thus he reincarnated himself as Josephine. . . .

When de Rochas had gathered enough information from and

about Bourdon, he decided to go back still further. After "magnetiz-ing" him, a new personality emerged in the foreground: a malicious old woman. Her name was Philomène Carteron and she said she was born in 1702. Her maiden name would have been Charpigny. Her grandfather on her mother's side was named Machon and lived in Ozan. In 1732 she married Carteron at Chevreux; she bore him two children but lost them through death. She could not write, did not go to church, and felt that death was the end of everything. . . .

According to Josephine, before she became Philomène, she was a girl who died very young. Before that, a man who robbed and murdered—a real bandit.

When de Rochas told his subject to return even further, she declared—hesitantly and her face shyly averted—that she had been an ape, big and almost human. Later on she stated she had lived still other lives one after another, between those of the ape and the bandit. In one such incarnation, she was supposed to have lived in the woods and killed wolves.

Naturally, de Rochas began an investigation at Ozan and Chevreux into the Charpigny and Carteron families. Although this research disclosed that both families were not unknown in these communities, he was unable to find an undisputed trace of Philomène.

Furthermore, the personalities which he uncovered in his other subjects could not be provably identified. For that reason, the re-searcher stated in 1913,[18] that his tests in the area of regression of memory should only be considered as contributions to our knowledge of secondary and tertiary personalities. "The reports about lives in succession, done with mesmerized subjects, offer too many well-established errors for them to be acceptable as direct proof of the existence of those lives."

We read in *Das Okkulte*, Darmstadt, 1923, by Keyserling, Happich, and Rousselle, that the first two[19] repeated de Rochas' experiments in 1922. Mr. H. B., who had demonstrated some degree of paragnostic capacity, was used as a test subject. Keyserling, who was not an ad-herent of reincarnation, called Happich's attention to de Rochas' work and they both decided to repeat de Rochas' regression ex-periment without the knowledge of the subject. It would be con-ducted by Happich, whose views on reincarnation are not known.

According to both of the researchers, Mr. B. did not believe in reincarnation nor did he know of the existence and contents of de Rochas' book on successive lives.

The first test was undertaken immediately following a series of psychoscopic experiments; the subject usually worked in a rather deep trance.

The tests were successful in that Mr. B., like the subjects described by de Rochas, was able to run through a few of his supposedly previous incarnations. According to his account, in a previous life he had been a man who was persecuted on account of unorthodox religious beliefs in the fifteenth century. He furnished ample details which, however, were inconclusive. In the next preceding incarnation, according to the notes taken down by the researchers, he was a woman who lived towards the beginning of the Middle Ages. He could tell considerably less about that life, however, than about the fifteenth century one.

The subject also reported various things about his experiences between incarnations. When we consider that Mr. B. was associated to quite some extent with spiritistic circles, this should cause us not to attach too much value to these reports. Recollection of what he read in spiritistic and theosophical books about the "hereafter" must undoubtedly have influenced him.

It should also be noted that these experiments seemed to make him unusually tired. Another remarkable fact was that the subject never seemed to remember anything about these sessions upon awakening. When, however, he obtained impressions in trance from objects (inductors), then he could often still remember the experiments a few days afterwards. The amnesia was thus much less complete in the psychoscopic experiments than it was in the research for possible remembrance of past lives.

Keyserling does not hold at all that these tests may be considered to be a positive contribution towards a solution of the question of reincarnation. He does believe, however, that if reincarnation should be a fact and the human should be able to remember something about his past lives, then the method used by him and de Rochas should be considered the correct one, if indeed it is possible to learn anything about our past lives.

The Bridey Murphy Case

Early in 1956, a book entitled *The Search for Bridey Murphy* was published in the United States and was a great success. It was translated into several languages. Its author is Morey Bernstein, an accomplished hypnotist of Pueblo, Colorado. In his book, he describes experiments which are basically similar to those previously mentioned, by de Rochas, Keyserling, and Happich.

He found a good subject for experimentation in Ruth Simmons, a young woman who seemed easy to hypnotize. In her hypnotic states, she recounted that in a previous life she was named Bridey Murphy and lived in Ireland. Data she supplied about this life in Ireland included some details which upon investigation were found to be correct.

Can it be accepted from this that Ruth is the reincarnation of Bridey Murphy?

The answers to this question differ.[20] Although some believe that Bridey Murphy did establish her identity conclusively, others see in Bridey Murphy the result of a dramatic splitting of the subject's personality, to which hypothesis they attach some psychoanalytic views. The fact that some details of life in Ireland in the middle of the nineteenth century can be verified might be explained by assuming that in her youth, Ruth Simmons had read one or more books with an Irish setting, so that the verifiable data could be due to cryptomnesia.

Retrocognition and Belief in Reincarnation

A Netherlander who emigrated to South Africa in 1897 and participated in the Boer War wrote me a letter in 1932 in which he reported[21] several paragnostic experiences he lived through himself. He described one of these cases as follows:

> ...A few months later our unit of command was situated by turns at Kimberley and at Modderrivier. Those days were dull. The horses had to be spared as much as possible because the fields in that area were very poor—they did not afford sufficient fodder for the thousands of horses—and transportation was also poor. Man and beast alike were starving. There was more than ample opportunity to

sleep, in the day-time, too, and as there was little or nothing else to
do, we all slept a lot, including myself.

I don't know why, but I always dreamed during the day, that our
commando moved on and on and on. Back and forth. Sometimes
fast, sometimes steadily. Then again, long treks, then again, short
ones. It was a peculiar landscape we were in. So totally different from
Standerton, or Griqualand, or Barkley West. Even different from
Wolmaransstad. I could not rid myself of these dream-images. That
was in November 1899 to January 1900.

Eighteen months later, our roaming started at Lichtenburgse. Then
I recognized the landscape of my dreams and took part in the moving
back and forth in that area: hunted by the British, then in turn chas-
ing them. Or, by sham maneuvers, drawing them away from our
armies with their attached women, children, and livestock....

Here we are dealing with an extension of the present into the
future. Contrasted with the extension of the present into the
future, or precognition, there is the extension of the present into the
past, retrocognition. The so-called clairvoyance in the present, which
can also be regarded as so-called clairvoyance in space,[22] forms the
transition between "pro-" and "retro-"scopy.

The next case will serve as an example of retroscopy. It concerned one of my subjects. In connection with a consultation for
police purposes one day, he furnished a description of the interior of
a cottage which, upon investigation, did not coincide with reality.
Further inquiry, however, disclosed that the description given by the
paragnost did coincide with the interior of this cottage about ten
years earlier.

The same paragnost, on the occasion of another investigation for
police purposes, was in a school building in The Hague. He suddenly felt as if he were placed in the past and began a detailed description of an old-fashioned sawmill. Although these data were of
no use for the purposes of the case on which he was being consulted,
one of those present decided to investigate the accuracy of the vision.
It turned out that before this paragnost had been born—and he was
then about 35—a sawmill had stood on the site of the school building.

We want to leave unanswered the question of the extent we have
to do here with "real" clairvoyance in the past,[23] but it will suffice to
point out the similar experiences could cause the people involved in

them to begin to believe in reincarnation. This happened, for instance, to Doctor X,[24] who while visiting a city in South Germany, where he had never been before and the history of which he never before had read, received a very vivid impression that, in earlier times, a cloister must have stood in the place of the hotel where he was staying. He could not rid himself of the conviction that he had lived in that cloister in an earlier life. This impression was followed by a no less vivid dream in which he received several rather detailed images of the cloister. An investigation instituted by him disclosed that indeed a cloister had been situated at this place in earlier days and that the visions which he had of it should be considered accurate.

Taking for granted that everything my informant told me here was true, which I am inclined to believe, and also that in this instance cryptomnesia is not a factor, which I think is probable, then there is still no reason for me to think of reincarnation in the same degree as my informant did. In principle, this case differs not at all from our first one, where, taking into consideration the age of the subjects, the hypothesis of reincarnation can be disregarded without much to-do.

The second case, also, which like the first one was thought of by the subject as a case of clairvoyance in the past, does not supply a sufficient reason for a parapsychologist to think of it as reincarnation. It may, however, be regarded as analogous to the first one. The difference between the two cases here lies only in the nonessential time distance.

The Case of Shanti Devi

As we have already seen, many people claim to have remembrances of past lives. Although, as can be expected, a great many such instances cannot stand up under critical investigation, a few cases are known which deserve our attention. One of these concerns Shanti Devi, the report on whom in 1936 by Professor Atreya,[25] who knew her personally, should be regarded as reliable.[26] According to our informants, Shanti Devi, who was born October 12, 1926, did not speak during the first year of her life. When she finally began to talk, she related that in the past she had lived in Muttra and had been a member of the "Choban" caste. She was supposedly married to a merchant of textiles who lived in a yellow house.

At first, her parents paid little or no attention to what they considered childish prattle. When, however, the little girl continued to talk about her previous incarnation, and asked them over and over again to take her to Muttra, they began to wonder if there might not be something "real" in her assertions. In 1933 Shanti Devi told her great-uncle, Bishan Chand, a teacher at the Ramjas school at Delhi, that her husband in a previous incarnation was named Pandit Kedar Nath Choubey and that he lived in Muttra. After considerable hesitation, the great-uncle decided to start an investigation. It then turned out that, indeed, a Pandit Kedar Nath Choubey lived there. He was told of the claim of the girl in Delhi. Contrary to the expectations of her parents and her great-uncle, the data furnished by Shanti Devi seemed to be correct. What with one thing and another, Pandit Kedar Nath Choubey finally asked his nephew, Kanji Mal Choubey, who was in business in Delhi, to interview the child.

After the parents had given their permission, the conversation took place in the presence of several witnesses. Shanti Devi immediately recognized Kanji Mal Choubey as a "younger nephew of her husband." She was able to tell of her husband, among other things, that he had an older brother, that her name was Lugdi, and that her father-in-law was still alive. Further, she described her home in Muttra and furnished still other "proofs" of her identity. These various matters are detailed in the brochure mentioned earlier.

On November 13, 1935 Kedar Nath Choubey came to Delhi with his second wife and 10-year-old son, whose mother had died and was supposedly reincarnated in Shanti Devi. When he entered the home of Shanti Devi's parents, she recognized him immediately. She was also very much interested in his son, whom she had brought into the world in her previous incarnation, according to her, after which she had died (the first wife of Kedar Nath Choubey had, indeed, died in childbirth). According to informants, the conversation between Kedar Nath Choubey and Shanti Devi was of such a nature that he was convinced more than ever that his deceased wife had been reincarnated in Shanti Devi.

When on November 15, 1935, Kedar Nath Choubey and his family departed for the return to Muttra, Shanti Devi strongly insisted on going with them. Her parents, however, refused to give their permission.

On November 24, Shanti Devi went to Muttra accompanied by her parents and several witnesses who closely observed the child. Her behavior was such that it was very difficult to overcome the conviction that in her past existence, Shanti Devi had been the wife of Kedar Nath Choubey. For instance, she seemed to know her way, with no mistake, in the home of this person. She pointed out, among others, "her former room." In this room she pointed to a place where she claimed "her treasure" was hidden, and was very disappointed when it was not there any more. Kedar Nath Choubey explained later to witnesses that he had removed the treasure following his first wife's death.

According to reports received by Doctor Walther from Professor Atreya, Shanti is still alive. She still remembers her "past life." She has not married, but has devoted herself entirely to religious Yoga exercises.

What should we think about all this? Even if we accept as accurate the reports received about this case—as a matter of fact not the only one—[27] then I believe it is still questionable whether we should take this as a "proof" of reincarnation.

Adherents of spiritism will ask, with knowledge of the case of Shanti Devi, if it is not more appropriate to speak of cases of possession in a spiritistic sense. They will point out also that the case discussed here exhibits remarkable similarities with that of Lurancy Vennum (the Watseka Wonder) to whom F. W. H. Myers devoted attention in his standard work.[28]

Mary Roff was born October 8, 1846 in Warren County, Indiana. She died in 1865 in South Middleport, a hamlet now part of the community of Watseka. Lurancy Vennum, born on April 6, 1864 was then one year and three months old. She began to see "spirits" when she was about 13. She also began to have fainting spells, which some people thought to be states of possession. Several doctors and pastors were of the opinion that she was insane and should be placed in an institution.

By coincidence, Lurancy's parents met the Roff family, who were able to persuade them to consult Dr. E. W. Stevens. He declared that Lurancy was possessed and gave her tests, the results of which strengthened his opinion that he was confronted with a possessed person.

On February 1, 1878 the deceased Mary Roff began to manifest herself, so it was said, through Lurancy. As it is termed spiritistically, she "took possession" of Lurancy's body, and according to informants, furnished the most remarkable proofs of identity. One of them was Doctor Stevens, who afterwards wrote a little book about Lurancy entitled *The Watseka Wonder*. This state of possession persisted for sixteen weeks. For most of that time she lived with the Roff family, who declared that it was as if their deceased daughter Mary dwelt in Lurancy's body.

Lurancy, as "Mary," was quite happy in the Roff household. She knew everyone and everything that Mary had known. As long as Lurancy was "Mary," she did not recognize any members of the Vennum family. Thus one day, at her husband's request and without saying anything to Lurancy about it, Mrs. Roff is said to have hung on a coat rack a little velvet hat Mary had worn a year prior to her death. "Mary" recognized it immediately, crying: "Oh, there is my hat, the one I wore when my hair was cut short." Thereupon, she asked for a little box containing letters. When Mrs. Roff gave it to her, she began to rummage through it. Furthermore, she asked for a collar which she had embroidered shortly before her death. In the same way, according to the informants, "Mary" recognized and was able to remember quite a few other details from "her" life.

On May 21, 1878 "Mary" said farewell to her parents and acquaintances and went into a trance, from which Lurancy awoke. If we can believe our informants, though, "Mary" must have manifested herself occasionally after that.

In 1890 the very skeptical Dr. R. Hodgson, as a representative of the American Society for Psychical Research, visited Watseka where he subjected all surviving witnesses to cross-examination. The results of this investigation were published in the *Religio Philosophical Journal* of December 1890. Hodgson found: "There is no question of a doubt that the facts were as described by Dr. Stevens" and he gave as his personal opinion that "the Watseka Wonder is one of the most impressive manifestations which plead for the spiritistic theory."

We can only point out that Hodgson made this statement at a time when the English Society for Psychical Research had been in existence for not quite ten years. If he had had at his disposal the knowledge and experience of the present-day parapsychologists, he probably would have been more cautious in expressing an explanation for the "Watseka Wonder," and also would have taken into consideration the possibility that Lurancy was a girl with a remarkable, but not understood, psychoscopic gift. Her phenomena might also be explained in animistic terms as well as the states of possession of Mr. C. H., which we discussed in *Tijdschrift voor Parapsychologie* XXIII, page 1, ff.

The same reasoning applies to what happened in the Shanti Devi case. Although I don't deny the possibility that we are confronted here with a case of possession in the spiritistic sense, and no longer stand *a priori* in dissent towards the possibility that in her past life Shanti Devi was Kedar Nath Choubey's wife, I still believe that the most probable explanation is that we are dealing here with a dramatized clairvoyance in the past, taking into consideration with this that in her native land the belief in reincarnation has a following of millions.* I gladly concede, however, that we cannot be satisfied with this admission. Although the results of parapsychological research compel us to take into account the unmistakable existence of something like clairvoyance in the past (an extension of our presence into the past) as the polar opposite of precognition (extension of our presence into the future), it still cannot be denied that we are confronted with many and enormous difficulties to explain this phenomenon.

We certainly cannot be satisfied with what Prof. C. H. van Os[29] and the engineers Dr. J. M. J. Kooy[30] and F. Ortt[31] and others have brought forth, with due recognition that our "naive" views on the reality of space and time are in need of revision. However significant the ideas of these authors may ultimately prove to be, we can at present say nothing more than that they are important contributions towards dispelling—somewhat at least—the dense fog enshrouding these problems.

---

* In his readable book *Die Seelenreise* (Olten, 1952), A. Rosenberg pointed out that we know of two kinds of "soul journeys." In the East, interest is predominantly in a belief in reincarnation: here we can speak of a journey of the soul through time, every time building up another body. In the West, under the influence of Christian views, we have rather been preoccupied with the journey of the soul through different spheres.

Chapter VI

THE QUANTITATIVE METHOD

Introduction

IF I place five cards, each carrying a different symbol, face down on a table, and I ask a subject to guess the symbol on each card, then mathematics tells us that theoretically the chances are that he'll guess one of five correctly, provided that he sees the cards only after the experiment is over.

It follows that if I take 25 such cards, five of each symbol, and shuffle them before the start of the test, I can theoretically expect the subject to guess five times correctly on the average.

Next, let us take two such decks of 25 cards and call them Deck A and Deck B. Now from each of the decks, properly shuffled before the start of the test, we select one card at a time, again and again—a total of 25 times, and record how often both cards turned up bear the same symbol. Investigation will show that this occurs perhaps five times, again four times maybe, although it might happen six or seven times. If this test is repeated hundreds of times, however, it will be found that it happens only rarely that the number of hits exceeds the average number of five.

It is quite different when several subjects, chosen at random (who are familiar with the symbols on the cards) guess the sequence of the 25 (5 × 5) cards in a deck, shuffled before the experiment. Experience in such cases reveals that among our subjects, there are some who, on the average guess correctly such an unlikely number of times, that it is mathematically out of the question to ascribe the results to chance.

Soon after the British Society for Psychical Research was founded in 1882, mention was already being made in parapsychological literature of the so-called statistical method. The first one to make use of this method in parapsychology was the French physiologist Charles

Figure 5. The symbols used on Zener cards are preferred by many over playing cards because they are not only simpler but pretty neutral.

Richet, who was always very much interested in parapsychology.[1] (In 1913 he was awarded the Nobel Prize for important research in physiology.)

If we are asked what led Richet to adopt this method, here is the background. In the early years of development of experimental parapsychological research, a few researchers attempted to establish the existence of telepathy by having persons who were believed to be "likely" subjects guess at drawings, etc. made by the experimenters when so placed as to be invisible to the subjects.

Although, as shown by the examples illustrated, these tests were often successful because the subjects apparently reproduced more or less accurately the drawings of the experimenters as a result of "impressions" received in a paranormal way, nevertheless some critics clung to the opinion that these results were not justifiable evidence of the existence of something like thought-transference or "telepathy." According to these critics, these results could only be called accidental coincidences. To silence these objections, Richet decided to adopt a method which might refute the criticism. He had recourse to a very simple experiment. He took a card from a deck of 52 playing cards, looked at it and simply asked the subject to call the suit of the card drawn. The chance that the subject would guess the correct suit was 1:4. Richet repeated this experiment 2,927 times with different subjects. The results showed that the suit was named correctly 789 times. Since the chance expectation of guessing correctly would have been only 732 times, there appeared to be a surplus of 57 times which, according to Richet, could be regarded as "significant."

Not only Richet but also others continued to develop this procedure. Over the years, numerous experimenters have utilized statistical methods in parapsychological research.[2]

The publication of J. B. Rhine's *Extra-Sensory Perception* in 1934, soon followed by other reports by this researcher and his co-workers, ushered in a new phase in parapsychological research which far outran all of the tests performed and reported on the application of the quantitative method prior to 1930.[3] Everyone familiar with parapsychological literature knows that the work performed by the researchers at the Parapsychology Laboratory of Duke University in

Durham, North Carolina, has been of such outstanding pioneering importance that many researchers elsewhere (abroad as well as in the United States) have been stimulated to follow their example. For the fact that the existence of extra sensory perception is today generally accepted as proved, we owe a great measure of thanks to the pioneering work of Rhine and his colleagues, yet not exclusively. The English researchers Whately Carington[4] and S. G. Soal[5] must also be mentioned in this connection.

Rhine and his co-workers have preferred to use the so-called *Zener cards* instead of the ordinary playing cards employed by earlier researchers. The symbols used on these cards are pictured on page 108. Designed by the mathematician E. Zener, they are preferred by many over playing cards because the symbols are not only simpler but pretty neutral. Some researchers have found Zener cards to become boring in the long run and have produced variations.

Some Dutch Investigations

In the Netherlands, Dr. P. A. Dietz[6] was the first to apply the quantitative method of research in paragnosis. Between June 14, 1916 and the fall of 1917 he performed a total of 5,996 playing card tests. Four persons served as subjects. So far as they knew, three of them had never shown any signs of paragnostic ability in their lives. The fourth subject, however, had apparently noticed Dunne-effects a few times in his dreams. The results of his investigations, which were satisfactory, were published by Dietz in the first year of *Tijdschrift voor Parapsychologie*. They were republished in 1936 in his book *Telepathie en Helderziendheid* ("Telepathy and Clairvoyance").

In 1920 Professor Heymans (Groningen) came into contact with a student of mathematics and natural science, who through sheer accident had found himself to possess a certain degree of telepathic receptivity. Because of this discovery, the student, Mr. A. v. D., made himself available for study. This investigation was carried on in the psychology laboratory at the University of Groningen between May 28 and September 10, 1920. It was supervised by Professor Dr. G. Heymans and Dr. H. J. F. W. Brugmans, who was to succeed

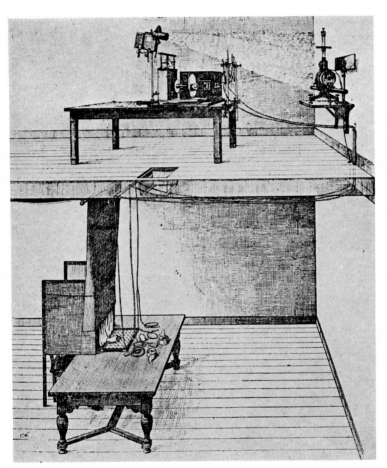

Figure 6. Groningen, 1920. This picture shows both rooms, one above the other. The subject was seated behind the screen. Instruments on the table in the upper room indicate when the subject has achieved a passive state.

Figure 7. View through heavy plate glass separating the upper and lower rooms. The subject's hand is visible on the board.

Professor Heymans as Professor of Psychology in 1927. The psychiatrist A. A. Weinberg lent his cooperation.

Because Mr. v. D.'s personality structure was exceptionally well-suited for the observation of the transference of motor ideas under experimental conditions, and the researchers rightly thought that the experiment should be designed to fit his personality, they arranged the tests so as to preclude any possibility of sensory communication from the beginning. Furthermore, they imposed an arrangement permitting an exact determination of the number of hits that might be ascribed to chance. By meeting these criteria, they hoped to investigate the transference of motor ideas.

For this purpose, a cabinet, closed off on three sides and the top, was set up in a room on the lower floor of the Institute of Psychology at the University. There was an opening in the front wall of the cabinet covered by a curtain. From the inside, the subject could extend his hand out underneath the curtain and move it freely over a sort of checkerboard which was placed there in a horizontal position. This board was divided into 48 (6 × 8) numbered squares.

Each test consisted in the experimenter looking at one of the squares (selected by lot) and trying to guide the movements of the subject's hand with his thoughts in such a manner that the hand would come to rest on that square. For his part, the blindfolded subject remained as passive as possible and, without being able to see the board, performed the movements which came into his mind. When he felt that he had arrived at the right spot, he pushed his finger down. Two types of tests, differing as to the location from which the experimenter gave his silent instructions (mental suggestion), were both used as much as possible during each session.

In the first type—the one-room tests—the experimenter stood facing the cabinet. Although invisible to the subject, the experimenter was no more than about a yard distant from him. In the second type of test—the two-room tests—the experimenter was in a room on the floor above the subject. So that he could directly observe the subject's hand movements, a rectangular opening measuring about 12 × 20 inches was cut in the floor, and fitted with two layers of plate glass separated by a dead air space. With curtains over the windows and the lights turned off, the upper room was in complete darkness, so that even if he moved freely in the room below, the subject could see nothing of what went on above him. The glass plates were so effectively soundproof that not even loud screaming in one room could be heard in the other. Since of course communication by touch was out of the question, the experiment can be said to have been designed so as to rule out the possibility of communication by any of the normal sensory channels.

Now for the results: in the most important two-room tests, in which the possibility of sensory communication was completely ruled out, the correct square was selected by the subject in 32 out of 80— or 40 percent—of all trials. The mathematical probability of this occurring by chance would be 1:48 for each separate attempt, because there were 48 numbered squares. Calculation shows that for 32 hits out of 80 trials, the odds that this might occur through chance are not more than one in 79 quintillion (1:79,000,000,000,-000,000,000).

On the basis of these results the researchers were convinced "that the existence of telepathy under circumstances where the possibility of communication through normal sensory organs has been completely excluded can be regarded as established beyond a reasonable doubt by these tests."

As for the one-room tests, in which tactile and visual impressions were entirely excluded, but in which auditory impressions (e.g. body movements and respiration of the experimenter) could be only partially excluded: here it appeared that in 23 out of 77, or 30 percent of the total trials, the correct square was indicated. The chance of this happening accidentally is 1 in 60 trillion (1:60,000,-000,000,000). With the weakened safeguards against normal sensory communication, then, came not improved, but inferior—although to be sure still very nice—results. This would seem to indicate that normal sensory communication plays no positive role in such experiments.

As has already been noted, the subject remained as passive as possible during the experiments. Brugmans wrote the following:

> This state seems to be essential in order for a telepathic transference to occur. This seems to be a prerequisite. The assumption of this so-called passive state is dependent to a great extent upon the will of the subject. In our experimental research, at any rate, it was a state which was always reached voluntarily. Yet this state was reached sometimes more easily than at others, sometimes it was toward the end, then again at the beginning of a session, or just the reverse. Sometimes the will seemed to be powerless, and then positive results also failed to materialize. The passive state, as a prerequisite for bringing about a telepathic transference, depends upon many factors, among which, however, the willingness of the subject is constant.

The passive state, in my opinion, should be regarded as a light trance, as indicated by the discussion in Chapter II.

Professor Brugmans was also able to establish by means of the experiment that the "feeling of passivity" which Mr. v. D. reported "indeed accompanies a changed state of awareness, and that the feeling is a very reliable indicator of that changed state of awareness." Use was made of the so-called "psycho-galvanic" phenomenon in determining this state.[7]

About 1950 Mr. J. G. van Busschbach, State Inspector of the Amsterdam primary schools, decided to undertake an investigation of school children. This inquiry involved the question of the extent to which a telepathic contact between pupils and teacher could be demonstrated by so-called quantitative methods. The investigation stemmed from the fact that several teachers claimed to have observed that they were often in telepathic contact with some of the children in their classes.

Plato had already reported that he believed he had observed that the students of Socrates seemed to progress more rapidly when they lingered in his presence. It is a likely supposition that telepathic susceptibility of various students in relation to their beloved teacher was the basis for this observation.

A teacher told Mr. van Busschbach that one day he hung up a blank map of the Iberian Peninsula. At a given moment he pointed at Barcelona, but as he did so he thought of Oporto. At the same instant he was surprised to see several of the students who were seated in the front of the class write down the word "Oporto," the city he was thinking of. And one of my subjects, who had already shown signs of a remarkable paragnostic power in his school days, told me that, without any effort at all, he frequently knew the answers to certain sums. On the strength of this characteristic, which they did not understand, his teachers considered him to be a "strange" boy. The result, moreover, was that he began to feel different from the others and thus seeds were sown for a so-called discouraging neurosis.[8]

Mr. van Busschbach conferred with teachers in several schools in his inspection area in Amsterdam and began to conduct tests in these schools. The classes tested were normal ones. He left the choice of teachers to chance.

In his experiments he had the teacher sit at the rear of the class, where he was hidden from his pupils by a simple arrangement of wall-maps. Next, the teacher was furnished with five cards, each printed with one of the following mathematical symbols:

$$+ \quad \mathbf{0} \quad - \quad : \quad \times$$

These cards were given to him, blank side up, by the experimenter. He then had to lay them face down on the table, in random order, without looking at the symbols. The teacher was also furnished with five smaller cards bearing the numbers 1 through 5. These smaller cards were to be laid down with the numbers showing, also in random order, on top of the five larger symbol cards. The experimenter remained in ignorance as to the sequence of both sets of cards.

Next, the pupils were shown examples of the five symbol cards which the teacher had before him. At the same time, the experimenter told them that their teacher would look at one of the symbols ten times, and that they were then to guess which of the five symbols it was. As a reminder, illustrations of the symbols were arrayed on the blackboard with thumbtacks.

Next, in random order, and following a sequence supplied by the experimenter, the teacher turned the cards over one at a time, focussing his attention on each card in turn. On forms provided for the purpose, the pupils indicated which card they thought the teacher had turned.

After the pupils had thus guessed the mathematical symbols ten times, they were required in a similar way to guess ten times among five colors and five words.

These tests were begun in Amsterdam in 1951. A total of 673 fifth and sixth grade pupils in 21 different classes were tested in the manner just described. In total, they guessed more than 20,000 times. Statistical processing indicated that the result reached a significant surplus of hits.

A similar investigation was carried out in Utrecht in 1953. This time the Parapsychological Institute of the State University participated, and I made available several assistants from the Institute. In total, 26 classes were involved in this research. Altogether, the pupils produced 26,880 guesses. Again a significant surplus of hits was obtained. Comparison of the surplus obtained in Amsterdam with that obtained in Utrecht showed that the two significant remainders were about equal.

Thus, in total, 47 classes were tested in Amsterdam and Utrecht. Altogether, these classes produced 47,070 guesses. Statistical processing of the data showed such a significant surplus (the so-called critical ratio in this total of guesses was 4.07), that the probability of obtaining such a significant total surplus by chance was practically nil. It may be said, then, that it is almost certain that in these tests a particular factor appeared to exert a guiding influence on the choice of answers by the pupils. Furthermore, where such a large number of randomly chosen subjects were involved that the individual factors were canceled out in these tests, we surely are entitled to say that, here, we are approaching a common phenomenon. With the increase in the number of guesses, this common phenomenon becomes increasingly evident.

Mr. van Busschbach observed quite correctly that the results of this investigation did not supply an answer to the question whether the children had any special telepathic* susceptibility towards their teachers. It was possible that children in the upper grades of the elementary schools might show a special "sensitivity" which would also appear in relation to others.

To investigate this, a series of tests were taken, completely similar to those described and with some of the same pupils who were involved in those tests. But, instead of known and trusted teachers, a gentleman completely unknown to the pupils, an assistant at the Institute, posed as the so-called agent. This investigation showed a noticeably smaller number of hits. Out of the resulting 21,570 guesses, a critical ratio of 1.9 resulted. Although this result was positive, it still could not be termed significant. This meant, then, that the person of the teacher obviously played a role in these tests.

Mr. van Busschbach's investigations, which were published in *Tijdschrift voor Parapsychologie*,[9] attracted the attention of Professor Rhine and his co-workers. As a result, they invited Mr. van Busschbach to visit Durham, North Carolina. With the cooperation of assistants of the Parapsychology Laboratory at Duke University, the tests performed in the Netherlands were repeated in Durham and nearby areas. The results of this American research paralleled those of the tests made in the Netherlands.[10]

Mr. van Busschbach also experimented with older pupils, in continuation classes and various secondary schools. The results of these investigations all fell within the range of chance. This is not surprising when we realize that, among older pupils, intellectual functions become more dominant. Here we approach a problem which was

---

* Where the teachers were shown the symbols, etc. we must take into account the possibility that clairvoyance of the pupils could have played a part in these tests. Only when the teachers had "only just" taken the symbols, etc. into their minds, could the factor of clairvoyance in space (the present) be ruled out.

treated by Ludwig Klages in his book *Der Geist als Widersacher der Seele*, and to which H. Bergson also directed his attention.

In 1955, Miss N. G. Louwerens, a co-operator at the Parapsychological Institute of the State University of Utrecht, undertook a related research project, although entirely independent of the previously discussed experiments, among a number of kindergartens in Utrecht. For this experiment an easily assembled portable screen was designed, consisting of three parts (a front and two sides). There was a shelf inside the booth to hold a book and signaling apparatus. The teacher could sit on a chair behind the screen, entirely concealed from the children.

The children, always in groups of a dozen, sat at small tables on each of which an envelope was placed. Each envelope contained 150 (5 × 30) colored prints. These prints consisted of pictures of a doll, a toy automobile, a ball, a deer (Bambi), and several cubes piled on top of one another. Each of these five toys had its own different color: Car—blue, doll—red, ball—green, cubes—yellow, and Bambi —orange with brown spots. The book on the shelf in the booth contained 25 (5 × 5) colored pictures of these toys. Furthermore, on the facing pages were black and white photographs of these toys. These pictures, which were considerably larger than those in the envelopes, were arranged according to mathematical principles.

The children were told to guess which print the teacher was looking at. She turned a page every time she was told to by a light signal. The signaling apparatus was operated by an assistant present in the schoolroom. When the teacher of these pre-schoolers had carried out the instruction, she would let the assistant know with a light signal. This assistant could never know which picture the agent had before her. Then, by means of a sound signal, the assistant let the children know that they were to "guess" the picture. They then chose, entirely independently of one another, one of the pictures contained in their envelopes. These had been emptied out on their little tables beforehand, and shuffled under Miss Louwerens' supervision.

A co-worker then went around to the children's tables to collect the pictures chosen by them in a box specially designed for this purpose. On the reverse side, the pictures bore an identifying number assigned to each child. After each round, the contents of the box

Figure 8. Stuffed animal.

Figure 9. Truck.

Figure 10. Doll.

Figure 11. Ball.

Figure 12. Cubes.

were handed to the assistant who manipulated the signaling device. He then filed the collected pictures in one of 25 envelopes on his table. At the close of the experiment, these pictures were attached to special forms carrying the name and number of each child, at the Institute. The number of hits for each child was calculated from these forms.

The instructions given to the children were in the form of a fairy tale. In this fairy tale, a little princess appeared who possessed a picture book, mixed up by the wind blowing through it. They were told further about a good fairy (her role being represented by the teacher), and the children played the parts of brownies who had to guess the sequence in which the good fairy had rearranged the pictures in her book. This was told to the children at the start of the experiment. While the teacher did this, she also showed them the toys. It was explained to the children that they had smaller replicas of the toys before them, 30 replicas of each of the five toys. The teacher also showed the children the "sealed" book, which she would not open until after she had retired behind the screen, where she would play the part of the fairy. It should be unnecessary to add that, for each experiment, another book was used, so that the teacher saw the pictures for each run in a different sequence. The books used were loose-leaf binders, so that the sequence of the pictures could easily be rearranged.

Miss Louwerens was always located at the back of the class during the tests. In this way, she could observe the behavior of the children, from whom she was hidden for the most part behind a suitable cardboard screen.

These tests were always repeated after a few days. During this second test, Miss Louwerens took the place of the teacher. The reason for this change should be evident. The object in view, among other things, was to find out whether it made any difference if a teacher or a "stranger" functioned as the so-called agent or sender.

Figure 13. While telling the fairy tale, a kindergarten teacher shows the toys to the children.

Figure 14. Before taking her place behind the screen, the teacher shows the children the "sealed" book.

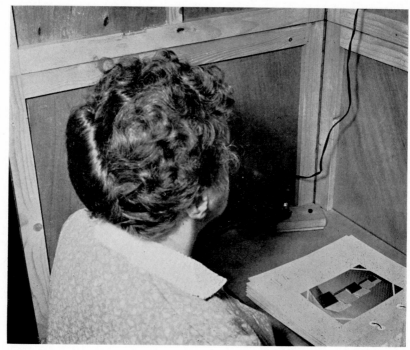

Figure 15. Hidden behind the screen, the teacher looks at one of the pictures in the open book. A part of the signaling equipment is visible at left.

Figure 16. One of the kindergartners slips a picture he has "guessed" into the box.

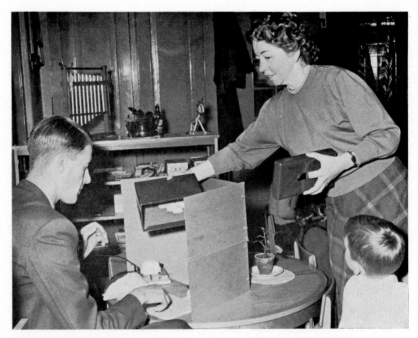

Figure 17. An assistant empties the collected pictures onto the table of a co-worker. Then he places the pictures into envelopes numbered to identify the turn.

Figure 18. The cabinet is dismantled after the end of the experiment.

Figure 19. Data obtained are recorded at the Parapsychological Institute.

Figure 20. One of the 1,188 drawings produced by kindergartners after the experiment.

Altogether, in this research 29 teachers and 1,188 small children were involved. They came from 15 schools and 29 classes. Because each youngster had to "guess" 25 times, the total guesses amounted to 29,700. Statistical processing of the material showed that the 1,188 children together had produced such a high number of hits that this could not be accounted for through chance. The chance that such a high number could be put in the category of accidental is smaller than 1 in 10,000,000 (critical ratio 7.47). Practically, the chance is about zero.[11,12]

Broken down according to the sex of the participants, girls were found to have produced as a group a significantly higher number of hits than the boys. This is in agreement with the results obtained by Mr. J. G. van Busschbach in the years 1956 and 1957 with pupils of the two lowest classes of the primary schools in Amsterdam and Dordrecht. Here he also found that the girls had noticeably higher scores than the boys. Running counter to this were the results of the already mentioned investigations among older children, where no obvious differences could be attached to the number of hits by boys as compared with girls.[13]

If we examine the results of the experiments where Miss Louwerens acted as the agent (10 classes), they show that the number of hits produced by the children could be ascribed without much difficulty to chance (critical ratio 1.54). This result favors the hypothesis that the affective fixation with the trusted teacher had a beneficial influence on telepathic communication.

Miss Louwerens conducted still another experiment along with this one, designed to obtain some further information about the personality structures of the teachers involved, and thus to establish the extent to which they might influence the results obtained.

For this reason, she had all of the teachers involved in her experiment placed under an extensive psychodiagnostic examination.

The results of this examination indicated that, on the whole, the motherly types among the teachers were those whose pupils collectively produced the highest numbers of hits.[14]

The So-called Quantitative and Qualitative Methods Compared

Although the application of the so-called quantitative method offers certain advantages and seems indispensable to modern parapsychological research, one should be wary of the all too one-sided application of this method, because, used exclusively, it only gives us an opportunity to investigate the periphery, and never lets us, as Dr. R. Thouless (Cambridge) once remarked, "plunge into paranormal depths." Compared to the experiments with psychoscopists of great stature, as I described in my *Beschouwingen over het gebruik van paragnosten*, the experiments reported in this chapter must be called meager in content. They remind us of the bloodless preparations on the dissecting table of the anatomist, lacking the signs of full life, which are shown especially in spontaneous phenomena and also in the phenomena which occur with the "great" psychoscopists. The application of the quantitative method does not bring us into contact with paragnostic phenomena which are a complete copy (in miniature form) of those phenomena which we encounter in the search for spontaneous paragnosis and in that of the psychoscopists. On the contrary, they are simplifications which differ qualitatively from the spontaneous and psychoscopic phenomena. The following will make this clear.

In his research into paragnosis, Rhine has not limited himself to applying the so-called quantitative method to telepathy and clairvoyance in space or of the present, but has also applied it to proscopy. In one of his papers,[15] he reported an experiment in which a number of subjects were instructed to place 25 Zener cards in empty compartments of appropriate size. After the subjects had complied with the instructions, a second series of 25 cards, the order of which had been determined by lot, were on a later date placed on top of the first 25 Zener cards. The drawing by lot was done after the subjects had filled their compartments with the cards. Afterwards, the number of hits was counted. With the help of these and similar experiments, repeated many times, Rhine and his colleagues succeeded in supplying a contribution towards proving the existence of proscopy.

Although the importance of these experiments is recognized, it must be realized, however, that they are incomplete. They need to be supplemented by similar tests employing the so-called qualitative method, like those undertaken by me, jointly with Professor Bender (Freiburg im Breisgau), with Mr. G. Croiset as the subject. These have become known as "chair tests." In these experiments, several hundred of which have been carried out over the years,[16] the paragnost appears to be able to supply data (some of them extremely specific) about people who, on a given future date, will occupy a certain chair, often chosen by lot, in a certain place, in a certain auditorium.

With several of Mr. G. Croiset's predictions, it was possible for me to subject the data he furnished to psychoanalytical study. This study brought out some unexpected contributions to our understanding of the personality structure of the paragnost.

Finally, it should be mentioned, as set forth in my *De Voorschouw*, that a synthesis of the so-called qualitative and quantitative methods can be accomplished. This has already been pointed out by W. Carington.[17]

NOTES

Chapter I

1. Prof. E. D. Wiersma observed quite correctly that psychic amnesias have a great deal in common with psychic anaesthesias; F. W. H. Myers, of course, was already familiar with this. In his standard work, *Human Personality and Its Survival of Bodily Death* (1904), this pioneer observed that psychic amnesia will develop when the attention is being diverted from events out of the past. Psychic hypermnesia, on the contrary, develops when the attention is focussed to excess on certain past events.

Now one can also, Myers says, direct one's attention away from certain present events, in which case psychic anaesthesia will develop (hysterical blindness, deafness, numbness, etc.). If, on the other hand, one focusses one's attention excessively on one or another present event, psychic hyperaesthesia will develop.

2. Heim, for instance, had the illusion that "the beautiful blue heaven he was looking up at, he would also find underneath himself, and he would very gently land in it." He also "heard" fine organ music.

Some of the informants reported that during their falls they had illusory sensations of having been in similar situations long before (sensation du déjà vu).

A. Adler's pupil E. Wexberg, in *Individual Psychologie* (Leipzig, 1928) page 36, takes the position that in such cases, the *sensation du déjà vu*—teleological meaning of the *déjà vu*—is a means of calming us down. "The fictive identification with an earlier event creates a calming and relaxing effect, all difficulties seem lessened . . . even that which has yet to take place seems to have been viewed once before."

3. Not all informants report a chronological order. Some of them claim that their past moved by their spiritual eye in a reverse order.

4. In the psychology of religion, the term *conversion* means a complete change of direction in life in the religious sense.

William James, in *The Varieties of Religious Experience* (Fifth
Edition, London, 1903), pointed out in relation to the psychological
mechanism of conversions that these result in most cases when impressions, inclinations, etc. which have accumulated in the subconscious emerge into the aware thoughts and feelings of the con-
vert. After a kind of incubation period, the unconscious tensions
become too great, and an "explosion" takes place.

5. F. W. H. Myers reported *Proceedings of the Society for Psychical
Research,* (Vol. XI, page 354) that once when Charles Darwin fell
off a wall, he saw several scenes from his book of life pass before his
spiritual eye with the most extraordinary clarity and vivacity. See
further A. Heim: Note 2 to this chapter.

6. By the term *heuristic* I mean here a useful, methodical way to
come to a deeper understanding.

7. It has happened to me personally again and again that one
or another image out of my own childhood years passed by the
spiritual eye of a psychoscopist. I have also observed this phenomenon
in my subjects in connection with other people.

A psychoscopist, being consulted by one of my acquaintances,
suddenly "saw" the image of a lady with a brown suitcase. After
mulling this over, the consultant remembered that a few days earlier
he had stood at a tramstop talking with a stranger, whose appearance
was as described by the psychoscopist. This lady, who had asked him
for directions, carried a brown suitcase.

8. This suggests that the informant, like most psychoscopists,
achieved a lowered and narrowed state of consciousness.

9. See *Tijdschrift voor Parapsychologie* ("Journal of Parapsychology"), Vol. XI, pages 209 ff.

10. I am reminded here, for instance, of C. U. Ariëns Kappers, a
brain anatomist who died in 1946 and who in his writings repeatedly
expressed his great admiration for Bergson's views.

Also H. Driesch, founder of neo-vitalism, has more than once given
evidence of his great admiration for Bergson's views in regard to
the function of the brain.

11. ". . . es wird künftig. . . noch bewiesen werden: dass die men-
schliche Seele auch in diesem Leben noch in einer unauflöslich ver-
knüpften Gemeinschaft mit allen immateriallen Naturen der Geister-

welt stehe, dass sie wechselweise in diese wirke und von ihnen Eindrücke empfange, deren sie sich aber als Mensch nicht bewusst ist, so lange alles wohl steht." (". . . It remains for the future. . .it has yet to be proved that the human soul retains an unbreakable connection with the immaterial spirit-world, through which by turns it works and from which it receives impressions; of these, however, the human is unaware so long as everything remains all right.") Kant: *Träume eines Geistersehers* ("Dreams of a Spirit-Seer"), 1766.

Chapter II

1. Some researchers believe that a distinction should be drawn between telepathy and mind reading. They claim that in telepathy, the subject receives thoughts emitted by the psyche of the consultant. In mind reading ("tapping the mind of another person"—Driesch) the subject draws on the psyche of the consultant.

2. See my *Parapsychologische verschijnselen en beschouwingen* ("Parapsychological Phenomena and Views").

3. Under certain conditions, some subjects show the inclination to seize their consultants' hands, especially when, as they habitually express it, they have difficulty in "making contact" with them. It cannot be denied that such bodily contacts can sometimes stimulate and enhance the performance of psychoscopists. Skilled professional paragnosts, however, very rarely show this inclination, and then only in exceptional situations.

4. It seems quite reasonable to suppose that the girl did suppress this memory. From the psychoanalytical point of view, it has been shown that the likelihood of a thought popping up in the consciousness of the subject becomes greater if that particular thought has been suppressed by the consultant.

5. Stephan Ossowiecki, an engineer, born in Poland in 1877, possessed a remarkable paragnostic talent. He frequently placed his performances at the disposal of scientific research. See K. Kuchynka: *"Der berühmte Hellseher Ing. Stephan Ossowiecki"* ("The Famous Clairvoyant Engineer Stephan Ossowiecki"), *Neue Wissenschaft*, 1955, pages 177 ff.

6. Because of the veridity, (pseudo-) hallucinations of paragnosts

differ from the hallucinations of the mentally ill, in which only their imagination or fantasies appear.

We speak of (*pseudo-*) *hallucinations* as long as the paragnosts realize that their "images" should be regarded as objectified ideas projected into the outside world. When they are persuaded to accept these images, etc. somehow or other as perceptions—in other words, to credit them with an existence independent of themselves—we then speak of *hallucinations*.

7. With Jaensch, we understand *eidetic images* to mean those memory images that show unusual clarity and detail. They remind us of positive after-images, yet differ from these fading phenomena by their psychonomic character.

Jaensch, who gave us his views on psychogenesis, was of the opinion that originally the eidetic disposition was an undifferentiated unity, and this unity was neither perception nor presentation. Perception, and presentation—which is reproduced perception—have evolved from this originally undifferentiated unity. From research carried out by Jaensch and his students, we have found that young children, many of them eidetically talented, often find it difficult to distinguish between dreams and waking reality. According to Jaensch, this is consistent with this undifferentiated unity. Ordinarily, this eidetic talent is observed to diminish and finally disappear around the age of 13 or 14. Research, however, discloses that it persists in some adults, whom Jaensch describes as cases of *fixation-and-regression phenomena*.

Eidetic phenomena are by no means limited to sight alone. Such pseudo-hallucinations appear also in other areas of the senses. See further my *Inleiding tot de parapsychologie* ("Introduction to Parapsychology"), pages 216 ff.

8. These secondary personalities repeatedly give themselves names. We call this dramatic splitting of personality. See P. Janet: *L'automatisme psychologique* ("Psychological Automatism"), 10th edition, Paris, 1930.

Such secondary personalities introduce themselves to spiritistically inclined subjects as "spirits" of the departed. In certain circumstances they will develop into the so-called guardian spirit of the medium.

In antiquity and the Middle Ages, because of the influence of prevailing belief in demons, they appeared as "Hell's spirits." This was especially true in the case of people who had strong guilt complexes with a resulting need for punishment. Also in our days, one can still observe something similar now and then. See my *Het Spiritisme*.

9. See A Mühl: *Automatic Writing* (Dresden, 1930). The author-ess, an American psychiatrist, reported in this work her successful attempts at uncovering the contents of suppressed complexes by means of automatic writing.

10. William Stainton Moses (1839-1892) was an English pastor who was known for his paranormal talents. See F. W. H. Myers: *Human Personality and Its Survival of Bodily Death*.

11. The dowsing rod also belongs in the category of the Ouija Board, planchette, and related instruments. The results all are based on the ideomotor principle. See my *Het wichelroedevraagstuk* ("The Problem of the Divining Rod"), The Hague, 1950.

12. A number of paragnosts (so-called magnetizers and others) seem to practice healing. It is a fact that some of these healers do have a beneficial influence on certain patients. Opinions to explain these beneficial influences vary widely. While some believe that the magnetizer is only a therapist working through suggestion, others hold that the term "suggestion" does not sufficiently explain what a number of magnetizers do. See my *Aussergewöhnliche Heilkräfte* ("Extraordinary Healing Talents"), Olten, 1957.

13. See G. Heymans: *Inleiding tot de speciale psychologie* ("Introduction to Special Psychology"), 2nd edition, Haarlem, Bohn.

14. For their part, these other psychoscopists observed "things" which escaped Mrs. S. For the specialized interests of paragnosts, see my *Beschouwingen over het gebruik van paragnosten* (Utrecht, Bijleveld, 1957).

15. Various authors have pointed out that in (auto) hypnosis we are dealing not with a complete but only a partial lowering of the level of consciousness. See my *Parapsychologische verschijnselen en beschouwingen*, pages 97 ff.

16. With some subjects, certain physiological phenomena that accompany a lowering of the consciousness level have been success-fully registered by means of instruments (psycho-galvanic pheno-mena). See among others H. J. F. W. Brugmans: "De 'passieve

toestand' van een telepaath, door het psychogalvanisch phenomeen gecontroleerd" ("Verification of the 'passive state' of a telepath by the psychogalvanic phenomenon"), *Mededelingen van de Studie- vereniging voor "Psychical Research,"* No. 7, 1923.

17. The word "trance" is derived from the Latin verb *transire* = going over from one state into another. The trance is a so-called second state. See my *Parapsychologische verschijnselen en beschou- wingen*, pages 97 ff.

18. See my *Magnetiseurs, somnambules en gebedsgenezers* ("Mag- netizers, Somnambulists, and Prayer-Healers").

19. In my *Beschouwingen over het gebruik van paragnosten*, pages 74 ff., the subject of thinking in images is illustrated with appropriate examples, indicating that paragnosts frequently misinterpret their images, to the sorrow of their consultants.

20. See my *Inleiding tot de parapsychologie, Chapter* 8.

21. G. Heymans: "Over de verklaring der telepathische ver- schijnselen," ("On Explaining Telepathic Phenomena"), *Mededel- ingen van de Studievereniging voor "Psychical Research"*, No. 10.

22. This confirmation does not necessarily deny the possibility that there is a paranormal endowment which may develop in connection with the future development of the human race. See my *Inleiding tot de parapsychologie*, pages 216 ff.

Chapter III

1. Heymans used the term *depersonalization* to denote "a sudden and usually transient state, in which everything we observe seems to be strange, new, more dream than reality; our own voice sounds strange, as if we hear it with someone else's ears, and on the whole we have the feeling that we are not speaking and acting ourselves but, as passive on-lookers, watching ourselves speak and act."

Negative memory disorders are closely associated with depersonali- zation.

2. An interesting example was reported by Lydia W. Allison in the *Journal of the American Society for Psychical Research*, Vol. XXXVIII. It concerned a Mrs. J. Scott. During the night of August 26-27, 1943, she dreamed that her nephew David's plane was hit by antiaircraft fire and he bailed out. On August 27, 1943

the nephew was reported missing by the American Air Force. Further investigation disclosed that at about the time Mrs. Scott saw her nephew jump from a crippled plane, it actually did happen. Half awake (Mrs. Scott talks in her sleep), she recounted her vision to her niece, Mrs. E. Renwick, who wrote it down. The following morning, it appeared that Mrs. Scott could not remember anything about this dream, which she had completely forgotten. Even later she did not seem to be able to recall it. This case of spontaneous paragnosis would have escaped notice if Mrs. Scott had not spoken to Mrs. Renwick and if she had not jotted down what her aunt told her.

Lydia Allison pointed out quite correctly that it should be considered quite probable that many paragnostic dreams have never been brought to the attention of researchers because the "dreamers" awake without remembering what they saw happening during their sleep. We are sometimes surprised that some particular event was not observed paranormally, but we generally overlook the possibility that we did indeed observe it, but could no longer remember it on awakening.

The question arises as to whether Mrs. Scott might not possibly be able to remember her dream under hypnosis.

3. According to Freud in *De invloed van ons onbewuste in ons dagelijks leven* ("The influence of our subconscious in our daily lives"), Dutch version, Amsterdam, 1916, page 287, one must surely have touched on something one has lived through once before when one has the sensation du déjà vu; one cannot consciously remember it, however, because one was unaware of it at the time. The awareness of the déjà vu is thus, in short, really the remembrance of an unconscious fantasy. There are unconscious fantasies (or daydreams) as well as conscious ones, as everyone knows from their own experience.

Freud's views on the déjà vu supplement those of Heymans.

4. The duplicates were meant for me. Dr. Kooy sent me copies of his dream notes for about two years, in order to give me an opportunity to control his research.

5. Dr. H. H. visited me during World War II. Through me, he met Mrs. v. d. B.-T., a psychoscopist who then lived in The Hague. On that occasion, she saw that he would work in the future with a

man whom she described rather precisely. A few years later, he realized that the psychoscopist had described Dr. Theodor Heuss, who was elected President of the West German Republic in 1949.

6. Reports by various researchers in spontaneous paragnosis indicate that they believe paragnostic dreams differ phenomenologically from "normal" dreams. See my *De voorschouw,* The Hague, Leopold, 1970, pages 93 ff.

7. The movement to the left could probably be considered to be symbolic of death. See W. Stekel: *Die Sprache des Traumes* ("The Language of the Dream") and *Rechts und links in Traume* ("Right and left in the dream").

8. See Note 6 to this Chapter.

9. Leibniz, in his *Nouveaux essais sur l'entendement humain* (1704), regarded by many as his major work, wrote of a conversation between two people. In Book II, Chapter 27,6 the author, speaking through one of the characters, says Man has premonitions of what is going to happen to him, but that these feelings are often too vague to be differentiated.

10. This is not at all an imaginary possibility. There are known instances of suicide caused by autosuggestive influence.

11. From Mr. Boschma's reports to me, it appeared that his mother repeatedly experienced proscopic dreams.

12. See Note 2 to this Chapter.

13. This opinion is wholly that of the reporter.

14. See my treatise on spontaneous paragnosis, *Tijdschrift voor Parapsychologie,* XXII, pages 5, 103 ff.

15. Although it is possible that Mr. X may have purchased a brown bag because of the prediction, the prediction as the cause for the occurrence of the event is not at all probable.

This part of Point 18 should not be considered separately, but in connection with the whole.

16. On the basis of experiences with various paragnosts, it is considered quite probable that suppression did occur in this case. See my *Beschouwingen over het gebruik van paragnosten* (Utrecht, Bijleveld, pages 98 ff.)

17. In a number of cases, psychoscopists without being aware of it appear to have predicted for consultants the futures they desired.

These pseudo-predictions, which are often quite remarkable parapsychologically, depend upon telepathy. See my *Beschouwingen over het gebruik van paragnosten,* pages 143 ff.

18. Compare these with the case reported by Miss G. M. R., mentioned in my *Oorlogsvoorspellingen* ("War Predictions"), The Hague, 1948, pages 79 ff.

19. See my *Beschouwingen over het gebruik van paragnosten,* page 130.

20. See Note 6 of this Chapter.

Chapter IV

1. Here we have to do with so-called psychic anaesthesia, which we must distinguish from anaesthesia caused by injury or degeneration processes of the nerves.

See my *Magnetiseurs, somnambules en gebedsgenezers,* page 82.

2. *Ibid,* page 99.

3. Dr. Gerda Walther, who has contributed a great deal to the progress of parapsychological research in Germany, comes from an intellectual milieu, where the names of Haeckel and Marx were often mentioned with respect. From her early youth, she had spontaneous telepathic experiences. These brought her very soon to the realization that the world view of the materialists is untenable. Between the years 1915 and 1923 she studied philosophy and psychology at the Universities of Munich, Freiburg im Breisgau, and Heidelberg. At Freiburg she came under the influence of Edmund Husserl, into whose phenomenological and ontological methods she tried to fit her experiences. See her *Zum Anderen Ufer* ("To the Other Shore"), Remagen, 1960.

4. Marie de Rabutin-Chantal, Marquise de Sévigné, born in Paris in 1626, was renowned among other things for the letters she wrote to her daughter over a period of more than 25 years. These letters still charm us with their wit and spontaneity.

5. See my *Magnetiseurs, somnambules en gebedsgenezers,* page 140.

6. See my *Het Spiritisme,* The Hague, Leopold, 1970.

7. It is quite obvious that similar veridical identifications deserve the attention of the psychiatrist, since they differ from the non-

veridical identifications which we encounter in schizophrenics and others.

8. J. Hyslop demonstrated by means of experiments he performed with students that when the living are trying to establish their identity to one another, they also, under certain circumstances, resort to mentioning "trivialities." See my *Het Spiritisme*, Chapter X.

9. *Ibid, controles en berichtgevers* ("controls and reporters").

10. See my paper on the paragnostic ability of Mr. C. H., "De paragnostische begaafheid van de heer C. H.," *Tijdschr. v. Parapsychologie*, XXIII, page 68.

11. Although I think it improbable, we still must take into consideration the possibility that the subject obtained her knowledge in a paranormal way (long distance telepathy) from the consciousness of Sra. Penoles or from other persons connected with this research. In this connection, attention is called to the results of an experiment by Prof. M. Valkhoff with the paragnost G. Croiset, intended to establish whether our historical knowledge might be enriched by the employment of paragnosts. See *Tijdschr. v. Parapsychologie*, XXIII, pages 103 ff.

12. The pioneers in parapsychological research in England, who founded the Society for Psychical Research in that country in 1882, undertook widespread research into the occurrence of spontaneous telepathy and related phenomena. As one of the first results of this research, there appeared in 1886 under the authorship of F. Myers, E. Gurney, and F. Podmore the work *Phantasms of the Living*. The contents of this book are still worthy of our attention.

13. Another important point of difference, in respect of phenomenology, between the hallucinations of the mentally ill and the veridical (pseudo-) hallucinations encountered during research into spontaneous paragnosis, lies in the fact that the veridical (pseudo-) hallucinations preponderantly bear an "alien" character. They break through, as it were, the train of thought of the hallucinating person, into which their contents do not fit at all. (Doctor Bowstead, for example, was thinking wholly about his game of cricket when his train of thought was interrupted by a "thought"—which turned into a hallucination—of his brother.)

The hallucinations of the mentally ill, on the contrary, lie entirely within his train of thought. They are, as it were, outgrowths of it.

14. The readiest explanation in this case is surely that the paragnost derived his knowledge about the earlier inhabitant and her environment from the psyche of one of the neighbors (telepathy or thought reading). The possibility also exists, however, that we are dealing here with a case of displacement into the past (retroscopy).

15. It is apparent that here we are dealing with a case of precognitive telepathy—the paragnost derived his knowledge from the *mémoire future* of one of the consultants.

16. F. Moser: *Spuk* ("Spook"), Baden bei Zürich, 1950.

Chapter V

1. *O, hoeveel malen als ik door Zuidlijk-duitsche steden schrijdend*
Opeens van binnen-uit—moest stilstaan, voelde ik: Hier geweest
In oer-oude eeuw reeds is mijn wezen als deeszelfde Geest...
En 'k hield de hand op 't hart, waar 't bloed plots vreemdlijk
gutste.

("Oh, how many times have I, striding through South German
cities,
All of a sudden felt inside-out, and had to stand still: Been
here before
In some primordial age, my being with the same spirit...
And I held my hand on my heart, where the blood suddenly
gushed forth strangely.")

2. Charles Dickens, *Pictures from Italy* (between Bologna and Ferrara).

3. See *Sonderheft Reinkarnation* ("Reincarnation Issue") of *Zeitschrift für Religions- und Geistesgeschichte*. IX. 2. Keulen, Verlag E. J. Brill, 1957.

4. In his book *Des Indes à la Planète Mars* ("From India to the Planet Mars"), Atar, Geneva, Flournoy introduces Hélène Müller under the pseudonym of Hélène Smith.

5. Although when awake Hélène showed no poetic talent, in trance she seemed to be able to express herself in verse. She made some remarkable contributions to our knowledge of so-called mediumistic poetry. H. Freimark devoted an interesting paper to the subject, "Mediumistische Kunst" ("Mediumistic Art") Leipzig, 1914, in which he tried to show what the medium and the artist have in common, and wherein they differ.

6. Flournoy undertook very serious analysis of the personality of "Leopold." As might be expected, he had to conclude that he was a creation of the "subliminal self" of the medium, comparable to the fantasy personalities of hypnotized subjects ("objectivation des types" —Richet). According to Flournoy, this creation was brought to life by autosuggestion, and also by the influence of her spiritistically tinged environment.

Although "Leopold's" handwriting showed characteristic differences from Hélène's (in style, as well as in the formation of letters and words), it also showed great deviations from original specimens by Cagliostro (pseudonym of Giuseppe Balsamo). Flournoy sought in vain for proofs of identity. When questioned about his life as Cagliostro, "Leopold" either answered vaguely or enshrouded himself in a veil of secrecy.

7. The fact must also not be overlooked that Hélène portrayed Marie Antoinette only as a French queen. The fact that she was an Austrian princess by birth and spent her youth in Vienna was completely ignored by Hélène. This can readily be explained. Hélène knew of Marie Antoinette only as the wife of Louis XVI, and virtually nothing of her as the daughter of Maria Theresa.

8. See my *Het Spiritisme*, Chapter XIII.

9. This comparison reminds us of the question posed by Heine in *Die Romantische Schule* ("The Romantic School"): "Is poetry perhaps an illness of men?"

10. I must not fail to mention the character of *Woutertje Pieterse* created by Multatuli. Decades before Adler made known to the world his views on inferiority complexes and will to power, Multatuli had Woutertje (whose mother knew all too well how to inflict a depression neurosis on him) compose a bandit song in which the "poet" himself was the bandit leader.

11. See A. v. Schrenck Notzing: *Die Traumtänzerin Madeleine G.* ("The Dream-Dancer Madeleine G."), Stuttgart, 1904. See also A. de Rochas: *Les sentiments, la musique et le geste* ("Feelings, music, and mannerisms"), Grenoble, 1900.

12. When she was about 10 years old, Hélène was attacked on the street by a large dog. A chance passerby chased the animal away but disappeared before she was able to thank him for his intervention. This experience played a big part in the subsequent develop-

ment of her belief in a guardian spirit. Later, when she was a few years older, her family physician took the liberty of kissing her. She was very frightened, and "saw" in the same moment (hallucination) the unknown passerby appear before her. In later years the stranger also "appeared" several times. After she joined the spiritistic group and became acquainted with "Leopold", she began to believe that the "appearances" were connected with him.

13. Hélène found in "Leopold" a heavenly bridegroom. Such heavenly bridegrooms are most likely to be encountered in cases of female mediums with an inner resistance to marriage.

14. Groningen, 1931.

15. See K. H. E. de Jong: "Leibniz en de reincarnatie" ("Leibniz and Reincarnation"), *De Nieuwe Gids*, December 1921.

16. De Rochas was of the opinion that the kind of hypnosis depended on the means employed in inducing it. He was an adherent of the *fluid-theory* and thus felt that more than a suggestive influence emanated from his passes. See my *Magnetiseurs, somnambules en gebedsgenezers*.

17. As we have already seen, it is not entirely certain that we have to do here with a true regression. As early as 1852, du Potet pointed out in his *Magie dévoilée* ("Magic Unveiled"), that, by suggestion, a subject can be made to behave like an infant, an old man, a dog, etc. The subject behaves the way he imagines an infant, an old man, a dog would behave.

18. *La Reincarnazione. Inchiesta internazionale.*

19. Count Hermann Keyserling was the leader of the "School of Wisdom" in Darmstadt. He opposed Oswald Spengler and sought to replace science with Wisdom. His colleague, Dr. C. Happich, was a physician.

20. C. J. Ducasse: "How the Case of "The Search for Bridey Murphy" stands today," *Journal of the American Society for Psychical Research*, 1960.

Ian Stevenson: "The Evidence for Survival from Claimed Memories of Former Incarnations," *Journal of the American Society for Psychical Research*, 1960.

Nandor Fodor: "The Book that Started It All," *Tomorrow*, Vol. V, No. 4.

21. See *Tijdschrift voor Parapsychologie*, Vol. V, pages 67 ff.

22. A distinguished and well-observed example of so-called clairvoyance in the present or in space may be found in my *Inleiding tot de parapsychologie*, Utrecht, Bijleveld, page 45. It concerns a locomotive engineer who paranormally witnessed his son's brutal murder at the time it was committed. It is a likely supposition that, preceding this vision, a telepathic rapport emanating from the son took place ("Hellsehen auf Ruf"—Driesch) ("clairvoyance upon call").

23. The possibility exists that such cases depend upon telepathy and that the paragnost thus obtained his knowledge in a paranormal way from the psyche of someone cognizant of the earlier situation.

24. The name is omitted at the request of the person involved.

25. Professor Atreya of the Hindu University, Benares, who is generally considered an authority in the areas of Hindu religion and culture, evinces a great deal of interest in parapsychological research. Shortly after World War II he visited the U.S.A. This trip afforded him an opportunity to visit Prof. J. B. Rhine in Durham.

Several European researchers correspond with him. One of these, Dr. Gerda Walther (Munich) was informed by him of the case of Shanti Devi. Making use of the data supplied by Professor Atreya, Doctor Walther wrote her treatise "Shanti Devi und andere Fälle angeblicher Rückerinnerung an frühere Inkarnationen" ("Shanti Devi and Other Cases of Cited Recalls of Previous Incarnations") *Neue Wissenschaft*, VI, No. 7, page 214.

26. The authors of this paper, which Doctor Walther obtained through the intermediary of the International Aryan League, Delhi, and which is entitled "A Case of Reincarnation," were three prominent persons. One of them, Pandit Neki Ram Sharma, is a well-known leader in the Nationalist Party. Prof. M. Sudhakar, M.A., National University in Lahore, supplied the report with an introduction.

27. In 1966 Dr. Stevenson published a very important book regarding the reincarnation problem: *Twenty Cases Suggestive of Reincarnation*. These cases form a nucleus of a large collection of cases of people who believe that they, like Shanti Devi, remember their preceding incarnations.

The author collected these cases in many parts of the world, which he visited. Many of these cases are very interesting. We are grateful to Dr. Stevenson for making a beginning with a systematic scientific research regarding this disputed problem.

28. See F. W. H. Myers: *Human Personality and Its Survival of Bodily Death*, I, page 336, London, 1904.

29. C. H. van Os: *Moa-Moa. Het moderne denken en de primitieve wijsheid* ("Modern thinking and primitive wisdom"), J. M. Meulenhoff, Amsterdam.

30. J. M. J. Kooy: "Space, Time, Consciousness and the Universe," *Tijdschr. v. Parapsychologie*, Vol. XXI, page 127.

31. F. Ortt: *Het probleem der ziel* (The Problem of the Soul") 2nd printing, The Hague, 1951.

Chapter VI

1. Ch. Richet: *Traité de Metapsychique* ("Treatise on Metapsychics"). Paris, 1923.

2. See P. A. Dietz: *Telepathie en helderziendheid* ("Telepathy and Clairvoyance"). The Hague, 1936.

3. Some authors seem inclined to overvalue the significance of the so-called quantitative method and to hold the opinion that scientific research into paragnostic phenomena dates only from Rhine's work. This notion is inaccurate. The so-called quantitative method is only one of the methods which can be employed in parapsychological research. Rhine and his co-workers have placed far too much emphasis on this approach.

4. W. Carington: *Telepathy*. London, Methuen, 1945.

5. S. G. Soal and F. Bateman: *Modern Experiments in Telepathy*. Yale University Press, New Haven, 1954.

6. A biography of this Dutch pioneer was included in his report, *Wereldzicht der parapsychologie* ("World-View of Parapsychology"). The Hague, 1954.

7. See G. Heymans, H. J. F. W. Brugmans, and A. A. Weinberg: "Een experimenteel onderzoek betreffende telepathie" ("Experimental Research Concerning Telepathy"), *Mededelingen der S. P. R.*, No. 1, 1921. Also, H. J. F. W. Brugmans: see Note 16, Chapter II.

8. See my "Bijdragen tot de kennis van de persoonlijkheidsstructuur van paragnosten" ("Contributions to the Knowledge of the Per-

sonality Structure of Paragnosts") *Tijdschrift voor Parapsychologie,* Vol. XXV, pages 117 ff.

9. J. G. van Busschbach: "Een statistisch onderzoek naar de vraag of paragnosie aantoonbaar is bij normale interpsychische verkeer" ("A statistical investigation of the question whether paragnosis can be demonstrated in normal interpsychic exchange"), *Tijdschrift voor Parapsychologie,* XX, XXII, XXIII, XXV, and XXVI.

10. J. G. van Busschbach: "An Investigation of ESP Between Teacher and Pupils in American Schools," *The Journal of Parapsychology,* Vol. 20.

11. N. G. Louwerens: "Paragnostische experimenten op kleuters in Utrechtse kleuterscholen genomen" ("Paragnostic experiments performed with children in Utrecht kindergartens"), *"Tijdschrift voor Parapsychologie,* XXVI and XXVIII. (This article appeared translated in *The Journal of Parapsychology,* June 1960.)

12. J. H. Makkink: "Statistische beschouwingen met betrekking tot het onderzoek op kleuters in kleuterklassen verricht" ("Statistical evaluation of the research on children in kindergarten classes"), *Tijdschrift voor Parapsychologie,* XXVI and XXVIII.

13. J. G. van Busschbach: "Telepathie in de school" ("Telepathy in Schools"), No. 742 AO-reeks, IVIO Amsterdam.

14. The fact should also be reported here that Miss Louwerens put each of the 28 kindergarten teachers through a test using Zener cards.

15. J. B. Rhine: "Experiments Bearing on the Precognition Hypothesis," *Journal of Parapsychology,* Vol. V.

16. See my *De voorschouw,* The Hague, Leopold, 1970.

17. W. Carington: *Telepathy.* London, Methuen, 1945.

BIBLIOGRAPHY

Bender, H.: *Parapsychologie*. Darmstadt, 1966.

Broad, C. D.: *Lectures on Psychical Research*. London, Routledge and Kegan Paul, 1962.

Carington, W.: *Telepathy*. London, Methuen, 1945.

Driesch, H.: *Parapsychologie*, reprint. Zürich, Rascher Verlag, 1952.

Eisenbud, J.: *Psi and Psychoanalysis*. New York, Stratton, 1970.

Gauld, A.: *The Founders of Psychical Research*. London, Routledge and Kegan Paul, 1968.

McCreery, Ch.: *Science, Philosophy and ESP*. London, Faber and Faber, 1967.

Murphy, G.: *Challenge of Psychical Research*. New York, Harper, 1961.

Neuhaeusler, A.: *Telepathie, Hellsehen, Praekognition*. München, Lehnen Verlag.

Pollack, J. H.: *Croiset the Clairvoyant*. New York, Doubleday, 1964.

Pratt, J. G.: *Parapsychology*. New York, Doubleday, 1964.

Rhine, J. B.: *The Reach of the Mind*. New York, Sloane, 1947.

Rhine, J. B. and J. G. Pratt: *Parapsychology, Frontier Science of the Mind*. Oxford, Blackwell.

Rhine, J. B. and R. Brier: *Parapsychology Today*. New York, Citadel Press, 1968.

Rhine, L. E.: *Hidden Channels of the Mind*. New York, Sloane, 1961.

Schwarz, B. E.: *Parent-Child Telepathy*, New York, Garrett Publications, 1971.

Stevenson, I.: *Twenty Cases Suggestive of Reincarnation*. New York, American Society for Psychical Research, 1970.

Stevenson, I.: *Telepathic Impressions*. New York, American Society for Psychical Research, 1970.

Tenhaeff, W. H. C.: *Inleiding tot de parapsychologie*, reprint. Utrecht, Bijleveld, 1964.

Tenhaeff, W. H. C.: *Parapsychologie*. Antwerpen, Standaard, 1969.

Tenhaeff, W. H. C.: *Het Spiritisme*. den Haag, Leopold, 1971.

Tenhaeff, W. H. C.: *De voorschouw*. den Haag, Leopold, 1970.

Tenhaeff, W. H. C.: *Beschouwingen over het gebruik van paragnosten*. Utrecht, Bijleveld, 1957.

INDEX OF CASES

GENERAL INDEX